MORE THAN SURVIVAL

*Prospects for Higher Education
in a Period of Uncertainty*

A COMMENTARY WITH RECOMMENDATIONS
BY THE CARNEGIE FOUNDATION
FOR THE ADVANCEMENT OF TEACHING

*A Commentary with Recommendations
by The Carnegie Foundation for the
Advancement of Teaching*

MORE THAN SURVIVAL

Prospects for Higher Education
in a Period of Uncertainty

 Jossey-Bass Publishers
San Francisco • Washington • London • 1975

MORE THAN SURVIVAL
Prospects for Higher Education in a Period of Uncertainty
The Carnegie Foundation for the Advancement of Teaching

The Carnegie Council Series

The Federal Role in Postsecondary
Education: Unfinished Business,
1975-1980

Low or No Tuition: The Feasibil-
ity of a National Policy for the
First Two Years of College

More than Survival: Prospects
for Higher Education in a
Period of Uncertainty

Contents

Preface

For a century (1870 to 1970), higher education in the United States experienced relatively steady and certain growth. For the prior two centuries and more (1636 to 1870), growth was not always so steady but it was, by many, considered certain. Now, for the first time in our nation's history, the prospect is that growth may be both unsteady and uncertain. This is a dramatic, even traumatic, change of condition.

This commentary, the first in a new series of commentaries by the Board of Trustees of The Carnegie Foundation for the Advancement of Teaching, discusses the decline of the old and the birth of a new vision of the future for higher education. Subsequent commentaries, to be issued possibly on an annual basis, will also be concerned with broad issues affecting higher education.

The Board of the Foundation selected this topic and has participated actively in the general development of this report. More specific responsibility has fallen on the Council on Policy Studies in Higher Education acting on behalf of the Board. A majority of the members of the Council are also Trustees of the Foundation. The Council, in addition to its assistance with the commentaries, issues reports from time to time in its own name.

As background for this commentary, the Council initiated several studies designed to gather facts about the current and evolving situation, and to place them in an historic context. The detailed findings will be published separately. The studies are as follows:

1. *New enrollment projections to the year 2000 using national, state, and institutional data.* These have been prepared by Daryl Carlson, senior researcher, and Margaret S. Gordon, associate director, with the assistance of Scott Wren, postgraduate researcher, Stevan Keram, senior coder, and Ruth Goto, postgraduate researcher, of the Council staff. These projections form the statistical bases for Sections 4, 5, and 7. Mrs. Gordon also prepared the cost estimates for a "universal access" policy.

2. *A survey of institutional responses to reduced growth based on questions answered by about half of all colleges and universities.* This survey was conducted by Lyman Glenny, director of the Center for Research and Development in Higher Education, University of California, Berkeley, with the assistance of John Shea, Janet Ruyle and Kathryn Freschi. Data from this survey are utilized in Sections 2 and 6. A special debt of gratitude is owed to Dr. Glenny and his staff for their cooperation in making these data available in ways most useful to the Council. Special visits were made to nine black colleges by Israel Tribble, intern, to determine impacts of the current general situation on these particular institutions.

3. *A restudy of nine major multicampus systems of higher education as they face the uncertain future.* Professor Eugene Lee, director of the Institute of Governmental Studies and professor of political science, University of California, Berkeley, and Frank Bowen, specialist, of the Center for Research and Development in Higher Education, University of California, Berkeley, undertook this investigation as a follow-up of their pioneering study of *The Multicampus University* for the Carnegie Commission on Higher Education. Observations from this study are one source of the comments in Sections 1, 5, 6, and 7.

4. *An historical review of American higher education since the 1930s to determine what lessons might be learned from previous periods of abrupt change.* This review has been prepared by David D. Henry, distinguished professor of higher education, University of Illinois. His views are one source for comments, in Sections, 1, 3, and 8.

The Council has recently issued a report on federal policies toward higher education and the recommendations in that report and in this commentary are consistent with each other. The Council report, however, contains the more extended analysis and the more complete set of recommendations on federal policies. It has been issued under the title, *The Federal Role in Postsecondary Education—Unfinished Business, 1975-1980*. It relates, in particular, to Section 7.

Council discussions benefited from advice on a draft of this report given by Frederick E. Balderston, professor of business administration and director of the Center for Research in Management Science; Lyman Glenny, professor of education and director of the Center for Research and Development in Higher Education; Eugene C. Lee, professor of political science and director of the Institute of Governmental Studies; John Shea, associate economist of the Center for Research and Development in Higher Education; Roy Radner, professor of economics; Martin A. Trow, professor at the Graduate School of Public Policy, all of the University of California, Berkeley; and David Riesman, Henry Ford II Professor of Social Sciences, Harvard University. None of these advisers, of course, is in any way responsible for the findings and conclusions in this report.

The members of both the Board and the Council express their appreciation to the staff of the Council for its contributions to the preparation of this commentary, and particularly to Earl F. Cheit, associate director, and George M. Hannen, intern, for their overall assistance. This commentary reflects the general consensus of the members of the Board, and no single statement of fact or opinion necessarily reflects the view of each member. It is presented as one of many contributions from many sources to an understanding of the evolving situation affecting higher education and to the development of effective policies in response to it.

The Board of Trustees
of The Carnegie Foundation
for the Advancement of Teaching

John G. Kemeny
President
Dartmouth College

*Clark Kerr
Chairman
Carnegie Council on Policy Studies in Higher Education

Candida Lund
President
Rosary College

Margaret L. A. MacVicar
Associate Professor of Physics
Massachusetts Institute of Technology

Sterling M. McMurrin
Dean of the Graduate School
University of Utah

Malcolm C. Moos
President
Center for the Study of Democratic Institutions

*Rosemary Park
Professor of Education
University of California, Los Angeles

*James A. Perkins
Chairman of the Board
International Council for Educational Development

*Alan Pifer, *ex officio*
President
The Carnegie Foundation for the Advancement of Teaching

Joseph B. Platt
President
Harvey Mudd College

Stephen H. Spurr
Professor of Public Affairs
University of Texas, Austin

*Also member of Carnegie Council on Policy Studies in Higher Education.

*Pauline Tompkins, *Chairman*
President
Cedar Crest College

Sidney J. Weinberg, Jr.
Goldman, Sachs & Co.

*Clifton R. Wharton, Jr., *Vice Chairman*
President
Michigan State University

O. Meredith Wilson
*Director
Center for Advanced Study in the Behavioral Sciences*

Additional members of the Carnegie Council on Policy Studies in Higher Education:

William G. Bowen
*President
Princeton University*

Ernest L. Boyer
*Chancellor
State University of New York*

Nolen Ellison
*President
Cuyahoga Community College*

Lois Rice
*Vice President
College Entrance Examination Board*

William Van Alstyne
*Professor of Law
Duke University*

*Also member of Carnegie Council on Policy Studies in Higher Education.

MORE THAN SURVIVAL

*Prospects for Higher Education
in a Period of Uncertainty*

A COMMENTARY WITH RECOMMENDATIONS
BY THE CARNEGIE FOUNDATION
FOR THE ADVANCEMENT OF TEACHING

We have seen better days.

Shakespeare, *Timon of Athens*

If the trumpet gives an uncertain sound,
who shall prepare himself to the battle?

I Corinthians

1

The Problem

Higher education[1] in the United States is undergoing the greatest overall and long-run rate of decline in its growth patterns in all of its history. It is historically more acclimated to advances:

- After more than doubling in the 1960s, enrollment growth is slowing down and is likely to reach a zero growth rate within a decade.
- The demand for additional faculty members follows the trend. It rose to about 27,500 per year in the late 1960s and early 1970s. It will approach zero in the 1980s.
- Promotion opportunities for younger faculty members are decreasing. A few years ago, less than half of all faculty members had tenure; now the proportion is two-thirds and rising. The higher the tenure ratio, the more the barriers to obtaining tenure.
- Faculty salary increases that once substantially exceeded rises in national levels for salaries and wages and in the cost of living, now fail to keep up with the cost of living.

[1] "Higher education" is defined here as the "collegiate sector" of postsecondary education—that is, public and private community colleges, four-year liberal arts colleges, comprehensive colleges and universities, and universities and professional schools. This commentary does not attempt to cover the "noncollegiate sector" of postsecondary education: proprietary occupational schools, other postsecondary institutions (recreational and occupational schools not eligible for federal student aid), and "other learning opportunities" (such as those offered by churches, corporations, and labor unions).

- The percentage of the GNP spent on higher education (not including capital construction and certain other accounts) doubled from 1960 to 1972—from 1.1 to 2.2 percent, but it fell to 2.1 percent by 1975.
- Federal research funds that rose at 8 percent a year in the 1960s, and up to 15 percent in single years, now are static in amount in constant dollars.
- New colleges were added in the 1960s at the rate of one a week; now, in the early 1970s, colleges are failing, or merging, or changing from private to public status, and the overall increase in the number of campuses has slowed down.
- Federal outlays for construction have been cut by 90 percent and construction funds from state and private sources have also decreased substantially.

Yet, when the adjustments are completed, higher education in the United States should still be a model for the rest of the world:

- A higher percentage of youth will attend college than in any other nation.
- Faculty members will be among the more privileged groups in American society and the most privileged in the world.
- In this country, more of the gross national product will be spent on higher education, and more will be spent on university-based research, than is spent anywhere else.
- Colleges will be located within commuting distance of close to 100 percent of all Americans, and will offer highly diversified programs.

The problem is, thus, not so much what may be at the end of the decline in rate of growth as it is the rapidity of the change, and also its differential effects, for example:

- More negative impacts on new Ph.D.'s than on young faculty members, and more on young faculty members than on those with tenure
- More negative impacts on liberal arts colleges than on community colleges, and more on schools of education and

Figure 1. Declining growth rates for higher education

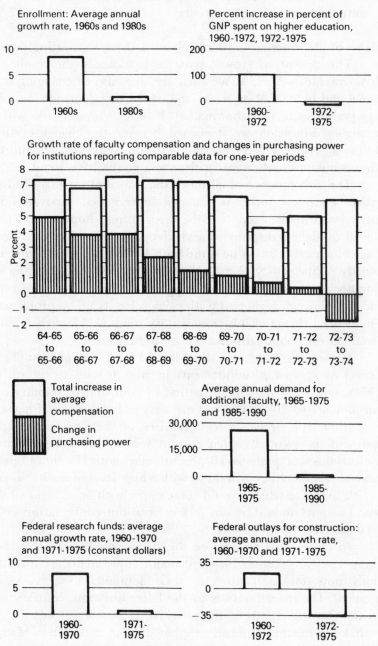

Enrollment: Average annual growth rate, 1960s and 1980s

Percent increase in percent of GNP spent on higher education, 1960-1972, 1972-1975

Growth rate of faculty compensation and changes in purchasing power for institutions reporting comparable data for one-year periods

Total increase in average compensation

Change in purchasing power

Average annual demand for additional faculty, 1965-1975 and 1985-1990

Federal research funds: average annual growth rate, 1960-1970 and 1971-1975 (constant dollars)

Federal outlays for construction: average annual growth rate, 1960-1970 and 1971-1975

divisions of humanities than on schools of business administration and health science centers

Many of the internal tensions relate to these contrasting fates.

The decline of growth patterns is basically the result of
demographic factors, as we shall see, but also of changing national and individual priorities and of shifting demands for college graduates in the labor market. Its effects on outlooks within higher education are deepened because the change occurs
during a period of recession and inflation combined. The short-
run economic situation intensifies the long-run basic trend.

The consequence of all this is that much of the higher education discourse today is couched in terms of survival. For
many institutions, survival is the main current imperative. But,
for all of higher education, the challenge is to do more than survive. Much remains to be done both by individual institutions
and by public policy to assure universal access to higher education to all persons and to enlarge the creative capacity of our
society, through higher education, to solve its many problems.
The central theme of this commentary, thus, is "More than Survival." Great public purposes remain to be served.

We see the future as falling into at least two phases: (1) a
period of downward adjustments in growth rates to the early
1980s, and (2) a subsequent period of comparative stability of
enrollments to 2000. The vast majority of institutions of higher
education will survive at least the first of these periods of adjustment in essentially their present forms, although there are
indications that perhaps 10 percent may not. The more open
issue is whether they will do so with a high level of institutional
health or not. Stability could come either with or without vitality. The goal should be not just survival but continuation as a
vital force in American society,

In our efforts to explore the future, we first look at the
current scene (Section 2): What major adjustments are institutions now making? How do their administrators view the
process? The overall answer to the latter question, contrary to
all the glowing visions of the imagined glories of a steady state,
is that administrators mostly view it without enthusiasm. Many

expectations for further rapid progress have been shattered, and some conditions have deteriorated absolutely rather than only relative to past hopes. The ability to adjust is being tested.

Second, we look (Section 3) at the recent past out of which the present evolved. What changed so suddenly? This is not to suggest that change is new to higher education. David Henry writes of the historic "constancy of change" in *Then as Now* (in press for the Carnegie Council) and the many prior "ups" and "downs." The current period is different in degree, not in kind; the preceding "ups" and the current "downs" are amplified beyond earlier experience.

Much of the anxiety now current is caused by the uncertainty as to when and where the decline of growth rates may end. Are we headed for an abyss, or will higher education rise to the stars? Both possibilities are now being suggested by highly regarded analysts of higher education. Our own prediction (Section 4) is for a relatively soft landing, not a hard crash. But no one can be sure. In particular, we have little past experience with unfavorable job markets for college graduates, and little experience with the related phenomenon of fast declining relative rates of pay for college graduates as compared with high school graduates. The yellow light of caution should be kept flashing.

We note one special potential source of danger. In the spring of 1975, applications for admission have risen substantially for a number of institutions. This reflects, in part, local circumstances and efforts. It may also reflect a tendency for young persons without jobs to continue with their education. Some people may, as a consequence, be led to believe that the 1960s have returned—like a miracle; and they may develop a false sense of future security. Thus, when the inevitable impacts of demography and the possible impacts of fuller employment assert themselves, they may not only be less well prepared than they could be but also may have taken expansive actions which will compound their later problems. The basic realities should not be forgotten in the euphoria of an upsurge in applications in a single year.

Higher education is made up of many separate institutions.

We group them (Section 5) into categories and seek to discuss what their separate fates may be. We find these fates to be potentially quite diverse. There are many fugitives, willing and unwilling, from the law of averages. Some institutions are undergoing fast deceleration of growth, which can feel something like fast ascent for an ocean diver, just because they grew so fast; others never grew at all in the 1960s. Also, if higher education were divided into teacher education (historically 20 percent and more like 25 percent if Ph.D.-training is included) and nonteacher education, then it would appear that the first segment has been decimated (actually cut about in half) and the second segment is generally healthy; in fact, some parts of this second segment are booming as never before: schools of mines and minerals, of law, of medicine, of business administration. Higher education stands divided against itself, part sick and part well.

What are institutions doing and what can they do to determine their own fates? We explore this question in Section 6. Certain themes stand out:

- The exploration of "markets" for students. So many institutions are now pinning their hopes on more adults; but it usually takes several adults, who tend to be part-time students, to equal one full-time student, and there are many noncollegiate competitors for adult time. But there are other markets too.
- The need for flexibility. Higher education is caught with many rigidities in a situation that calls for some fluidity.
- The importance of a sense of mission, an identity, a separate character; and thus of self-analysis and the development of a coherent strategy.
- The ability and the desire to compete for funds and for students.
- The search for greater productivity as against the cost pass-through practices of earlier times.

One overriding theme is more "administrative muscle" to shift resources and to make better use of them. Departments, in the process, may suffer, and they have been the most powerful centers of authority in many institutions. They have tended to make decisions on the basis of external intellectual developments in their own fields of specialization and on internal departmental relationships. Now the cold pressure of financial stringency is exerted from above. The process of decision-making is less academic. The day of the dominance of the department may be fading.

Much of the future course for individual institutions will depend on the wisdom and the leadership of presidents and the trustees who select and support them. A word of warning may be in order. Presidential tenures may, in practice, be becoming too short for their incumbents to be effective in long-range analyses, planning, and administration. Too much of a president's tenure may be taken up by learning the job, trying to survive in it, and then getting ready to leave it. Long-range problems of adjustment take longer-range leadership than the now-frequent five years or less.

For higher education to remain fully vital requires effective public policies as well as individual institutional efforts. The nation has a great stake in the vitality of its system of education. In the narrow sense of national income per person employed, "education per worker" has contributed about 20 percent (1929 to 1969) and "advances in knowledge" about 50 percent to the increases that have taken place. More "capital" and "improved resource allocation" are the other major positive forces at work, as against negative forces like fewer hours of work (Denison, 1974). Higher education contributes teacher training to all of education and is central to "advances in knowledge," and more income per person employed creates the possibilities of better health and a generally higher quality of life for individuals. Higher education is also a major avenue to greater equality of opportunity, increasingly traveled by those whose origins are in low-income families and by those who are women and members of minority groups. The participants within higher education are, additionally, a great source for the self-renewal of American society as they examine it and make proposals for its improvement.

We make three major suggestions for public policy (Section 7) to make good use of the capacities of higher education to aid the nation in achieving its goals:

- Financial provision to allow universal access to higher education (which is quite different from universal attendance, which we do not foresee)
- Steady support, at adequate levels, for the research and research training functions of higher education
- Support for the private sector of higher education as a good investment in diversity and in competition for the public sector

We also suggest that the states consider the possibility of using the current capacity of higher education to produce more specially trained teachers as a means of improving now neglected areas of schooling.

We warn, however, against trying to exercise too much centralized control by public authority either directly or indirectly through multicampus systems of higher education. A survey of the opinion of high officials of multicampus systems documents the trend toward centralization and more stringent review in many aspects of higher education. This survey was conducted by Eugene Lee and Frank Bowen in the course of a study (*The Unsteady State: The Multicampus University in the 1980s,* in press for the Carnegie Council) of recent developments in nine multicampus systems. Lee and Bowen judge that multicampus leaders are sensitive to these trends and are handling them with sophistication. But there are many unsolved governance questions of how to combine the knowledge of the "insiders" with the broader perspectives of the "outsiders," and of how to associate student interests and faculty expertise with managerial imperatives.

Finally, Section 8 is a summary that looks at the dangers and the opportunities ahead, the assets and liabilities of higher education in facing its future, and what most needs to be done.

2

Initial Responses to Reduced Growth

Although the full effects of declining rates of enrollment growth cannot be known for at least another decade, this new condition of higher education has stimulated a variety of predictions. Some of these predictions are that the effects will be wholly beneficial; but these predictions are seldom made by those most directly and immediately affected.

Observers with optimistic views employ arguments similar to those made in support of a no-growth possibility for the economy as a whole, some of which were first developed by John Stuart Mill: life will be qualitatively better, simpler, and more purposeful. Mill envisaged a world without "bustle," but not without qualitative improvement. In a passage quoted with approval by advocates of no-growth, Mill wrote in 1857 that ". . . a stationary condition of capital and population implies no stationary state of human improvement. There would be as much scope as ever for all kinds of mental culture, and moral and social progress; as much room for improving the Art of Living and much more likelihood of its being improved" (Mill, 1908, pp. 39-40).

The new condition, writes Robert Nisbet (1974), will pull higher education down from a "bogus loftiness" and away from what he calls its "nationalism," and leave it a smaller, more secure intellectual community for teaching and scholarship, and more concentrated on local relationships and considerations. Edward Shils (1974) contends that universities were weakened by growth and the new functions that accompanied it. Their future strength, he believes, depends on their returning emphasis to the traditional functions of ". . . instruction of undergraduates in the basic knowledge contained in particular 'disciplines,' the training of a relatively small number of graduates in research to be pursued later in careers in universities, medicine and industry; and the training of young persons for certain professions."

Those who were dismayed by campus disruptions in the late 1960s and believed that they were a symptom of the deeper problems caused by rapid growth will find the new prospect especially appealing.

There is no reason to believe that intellectual growth could not flourish in a "high level steady state"[1] in which higher education was freed from the burdens of growth and still could reallocate its resources as needed. Faculty energies previously devoted to recruitment of new faculty and to the addition of new programs could be focused on developing the faculty and program resources already available and on creating a better learning environment. Some institutions, as we shall note, have, in fact, set limits on their enrollments, though not on their incomes, and, at the same time, managed to progress.

[1]We do not, in this commentary, make much use of the phrase *steady state*, although this is the common code word for the period ahead. Technically, the phrase *steady state* means an absolutely fixed totality of elements, and this may or may not come to be the actual situation—more possibly not. There may be some steady-state situations ahead, under certain conditions, but this is by no means certain; it depends on many things, some of which we discuss. More colloquially, *steady state* implies a period of no change, and much will be changing even if the totality of elements (particularly enrollments) should remain the same—uncertainty will be more a mark of the period ahead than steadiness. Steadiness implies balance, and there will be many imbalances; it implies an equable situation, and there will be some convulsions. When we do use the term *steady state*, it is to describe a period of stable or slowly rising total enrollments as contrasted, for example, with rapid growth or rapid decline; we use it as a synonym for no growth or slow growth in total enrollments. We will also make reference to a qualitative "high level steady state" which combines important elements of progress within the context of no or slow growth.

Early Experiences

Favorable expectations contrast sharply with the responses to reduced growth of those who directly confront its early effects. Instead of a more secure community, a Council-sponsored study finds disappointment, conflict, fears of rigidity, and, increasingly, concerns about the ability of some institutions to survive.

The plight of the young Ph.D., fully trained, who cannot find an academic job is by now familiar. Somewhat less visible, though no less serious, is the disappointment of potential students who had hoped to enroll, but who cannot now do so for economic reasons. Their inability to enroll is, of course, one reason why enrollment growth is declining. The disappointments of administrators, whose hopes for the advancement of their institutions have been eclipsed by efforts to keep them from failing, are also by now a well-reported phenomenon.

On most campuses, however, the immediate prospect is not one of failure, but of difficult adjustments.

These adjustments are likely to be particularly severe for new entrants into the faculty labor market. A slowdown in growth might not, at first glance, appear to have a severe effect on demand for faculty. Overall enrollment is still growing, albeit at a slower rate. But, in fact, the demand for additional faculty depends not so much on the current level of enrollment as on the change in the prospective level of enrollment. When the rate of growth increases, the demand for additional faculty grows, and, indeed, grows faster than enrollment. When the rate of growth declines, the demand for additional faculty will fall, even though there is still some enrollment growth. A small change in the total level induces a big change in new inputs. Current hiring anticipates future needs.

The effects of deceleration in the academic labor market may be explained as follows: The demand for new faculty may be seen as being made up of replacement needs and of changes in the total stock of faculty. Because the present transition to no-growth occurs at a time of general recession and there is a reduction in net outflow of faculty members, replacement demand will probably be slightly less than would otherwise be the case. Also, the outflow due to retirement is at a low level—

half of all faculty members were first hired in the 1960s and
will not reach retirement age until about the year 2000. But the
effect of the change in the total stock of faculty required is
even more dramatic. When the rate of enrollment growth declines, the desired demand for additions to faculty stock may
drop to zero.

Figure 2 illustrates this effect based on calculations in a
forthcoming study undertaken earlier for the Carnegie Commission by Roy Radner and Leonard Miller (Radner and Miller, in
press, Chapter 9). It shows the estimated relationship of demand for new faculty to projected enrollment. It does not show
total need but, instead, additional current demand for doctoral
faculty.

Figure 2. Projection of new faculty needed at the doctoral level

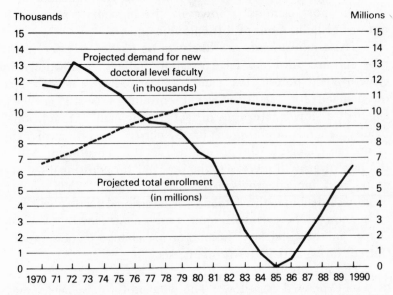

Source: Adapted from R. Radner and L. S. Miller (in press).

The figure indicates that the demand for new doctoral faculty will decline precipitously in the mid-seventies, reaching a
low of near zero in the middle 1980s. Subsequently, the shock
is absorbed, and demand becomes replacement demand which
rises with the rising age level of the professoriate.

The projections, as the Radner-Miller study recognizes, could be changed by many factors, including most importantly, changes in private and public policy.[2] What it does show clearly, however, is that the problems of adjustment are severe during a period of transition from rapid growth to reduced and then to no-growth.

Adjustment Problems

Decline in growth means that problems which might otherwise have been bypassed must now be solved. During growth, new space was available for new uses; faculty members whose fields did not fit changing student demand could, nevertheless, continue their work or find attractive opportunities elsewhere; new faculty members could be hired to teach in the fields of greatest demand. Now there are serious adjustment problems, physical and human. Old space must be converted. Faculty members whose fields are no longer in demand are denied tenure or are induced to change their fields of specialization; and prospective new faculty members, including women and members of minority groups, are turned away.

As the means to bypass these kinds of problems diminish, the old and new problems together tend to create an atmosphere of suspicion and conflict. The humane qualities of academic communities are being put to serious test. Colleges and universities in every section of the country have already experienced conflict about tenure regulations and their application; about hiring, promotion, and retention of professors; and about efforts to reallocate funds through termination of a once popular institute or program of study. More of these conflicts can be expected.

Some of the conflict is caused by attempts to avoid rigidity by changing tenure rules, tightening employment practices, and revising budget policies. As college administrators look at their rising tenure ratios and their tightening budgets, they are

[2] The Radner-Miller study demonstrates how this demand for new faculty might also respond to various policy changes concerning faculty-student ratios, the percentage of new faculty with a doctoral degree, and the distribution of enrollments among the different sectors of higher education.

forced to make (or plan) a series of moves that reveal the problems of reduced growth. They are predicting more centralization of authority; an increase in the number of students per faculty member; and a decline in quality of programs, students, and, to a lesser extent, faculty.

The intensified struggle for authority. Responses from campus administrators indicate that declining rates of enrollment growth are creating authority struggles. Administrators report (see Table 1) that, in the past six years, authority has already shifted from lower to higher levels. And, between 1974 and 1980, they expect that authority will continue to shift in the same direction. These are not the only changes in authority structures. The growing interest in collective bargaining adds another element of potential conflict. Collective bargaining is, in effect, a faculty-induced centralization of authority in a context of confrontation. Authority is seldom given up readily or seized without a struggle. The strong tendency in higher education under current conditions is for authority that traditionally has been widely dispersed within and among institutions to be more highly concentrated.

Increase in students-to-faculty ratio. Responses to the Berkeley Center Survey, undertaken on behalf of the Carnegie Council,[3] and discussed in a new book, *Presidents Confront Reality: From Edifice Complex to University Without Walls,* show that administrators from over one-third of all institutions of higher education plan a change in the students-to-faculty ratio—by implication, an increase in it. The planned changes, as Table 2 shows, are remarkably consistent in all categories of institutions. An increase in this ratio is customarily viewed within higher education as a deterioration in quality. Low students-to-faculty ratios have been cherished "givens" in many institutions of higher education. As they rise, faculty workload rises. Also, opportunities for appointment of new faculty members decrease, and the average age of the faculty rises. The amount of

[3]For a description of this survey, see Appendix A.

Table 1. Shifts in authority from 1968-1974 and anticipated for 1974-1980[a]

	Universities		Comprehensive colleges and universities		Liberal arts colleges			Two-year colleges	
	Public	Private	Public	Private	Public	Private I	Private II	Public	Private
From department to campus administration									
1968-1974	25	24	22	26	32	19	20	20	21
1974-1980	35	23	24	28	16	14	24	20	19
From campus to system board									
1968-1974	49	33	55	25	53	7	20	29	27
1974-1980	47	17	44	20	16	4	16	34	14
From system board to coordinating agency									
1968-1974	50	0	46	9	57	20	6	31	0
1974-1980	71	0	59	27	36	36	16	47	14

[a]Percentage of administrators who indicated a shift of authority in the specified direction.

Source: Berkeley Center Survey. (Liberal Arts Colleges I are highly selective; Liberal Arts Colleges II are less highly selective. See Carnegie Commission on Higher Education, *A Classification of Institutions of Higher Education*, 1973a.)

Table 2. Planned changes in students-to-faculty ratio[a]

| | Universities | | Comprehensive colleges and universities | | Liberal arts colleges | | | Two-year colleges | |
	Public	Private	Public	Private	Public	Private I	Private II	Public	Private
Yes	30	29	35	41	39	39	48	30	36
No	70	60	64	58	61	59	51	68	64
Maybe	0	11	1	1	0	2	1	2	0

[a]Percentage of administrators who answered "yes," "no," or "maybe" to a question on whether they planned a change in the students-to-faculty ratio.

Source: Berkeley Center Survey.

faculty time available per student tends to go down. There is no clear proof, however, that moderately higher ratios necessarily reduce academic quality.

The methods of adjustment to higher ratios that are most often cited are larger class size, increased use of paraprofessionals, and, to a lesser extent, more media-based instruction techniques. One of the largest of the state universities, for example, has already seen its faculty-to-students ratio deteriorate by 20 percent over the past eight years. A few of the administrators, particularly from research and doctoral-granting institutions, indicated, however, that they hope to increase the ratio of faculty members to students to counter the effects of increases in the number of students per faculty member forced by recent economies. There is no way to evaluate the ability of these institutions to carry out this hope.

Impairment of quality. Administrators responding to the Berkeley Center Survey indicate that the leveling of enrollment and funding impairs the quality of their programs, their students, and, to a lesser degree, their faculties. As Table 3 shows, just under two-thirds of public and one-half of private institutions report a decline in the quality of their programs. One administrator of a public research institution writes that: ". . . enrollments and funds have plateaued" and that this will ". . . impair the overall quality of programs. Already we have begun to experience this decline."

Administrators at both public and private institutions report that the quality of their students is already impaired. Administrators at private institutions believe they are particularly hard hit. At all categories of private institutions, in greater proportion than public, administrators contend that the leveling of enrollment and funding is responsible for a decline in student quality. A main factor, they report, is the rising cost of college education. "Many good students aren't enrolling because they just can't afford it," one college official writes. Another significant factor is the lowering of admission standards to raise the level of enrollments. One private liberal arts college administrator writes: ". . . as the level of enrollment drops it is inevitable that we are less selective in admitting students."

Table 3. The impact of the leveling of enrollment and funding on the quality of programs, students, and faculty

Percentage of administrators responding "impairs"

	Universities		Comprehensive colleges and universities		Liberal arts colleges			Two-year colleges	
	Public	Private	Public	Private	Public	Private I	Private II	Public	Private
Programs	69	49	67	40	50	52	49	54	50
Students	40	50	47	57	46	55	49	34	53
Faculty	60	46	55	33	15	35	46	43	37

Percentage of administrators responding "enhances"

	Universities		Comprehensive colleges and universities		Liberal arts colleges			Two-year colleges	
	Public	Private	Public	Private	Public	Private I	Private II	Public	Private
Programs	22	24	20	44	50	22	37	37	31
Students	32	17	23	25	31	19	30	37	28
Faculty	30	27	34	47	69	35	36	38	37

Source: Berkeley Center Survey.

Asked whether there is a decrease in faculty quality, administrators' perceptions are mixed. On the one hand, faculties, sensing the difficulties of financial exigency, are exerting greater effort in their instruction and research. The oversupplied job market also allows greater selection and thus yields more well-trained replacements than were available in the sixties. On the other hand, with less turnover, fewer vacancies occur. A large supply of well-trained potential faculty is of little benefit if there are no positions for them to fill. For institutions with rising tenure ratios, faculty-hiring decisions made during the "golden years," when students were plentiful and faculty were in short supply, lead to long-run problems of faculty quality in the 1970s and beyond. A static and aging faculty also is less responsive to rapidly changing student interests by field of study. Public research universities seem to feel that they are particularly affected by these problems.

Favorable Past Experiences of Individual Institutions

This pessimistic picture contrasts sharply with both the more optimistic predictions about the benefits of steady state, and with the past successful experiences of certain individual colleges and universities that have had little or no growth. Some institutions, in times past, have set a limit to their enrollment growth and have operated at that limit without serious problems. Why should there be problems now? The reasons can be shown by considering two different types of institutions: in 1965, Gettysburg, a small private liberal arts college, set an enrollment limit of 1,800 students (its enrollment had been 1,250 in 1954 and 1,500 in 1960); in 1957, the Berkeley campus of the University of California set an enrollment limit of 27,500. Both managed to progress.

There are at least five important differences between the situation these and other institutions with enrollment limits faced in the past and the one that is now evolving.

First, the enrollment limits in these individual institutions were planned and the institutions grew until, gradually, the target was met. The adjustments that had to be made were planned and achieved through slow growth, over a period long enough to permit the institutions to make the necessary accommodations.

Second, the process of gradual adjustment to a planned growth limit occurred in the larger context of growth in higher education and in the economy as well. This general growth meant that enrollment ceilings of individual institutions could be lifted, formally or informally, when necessary. At Berkeley, enrollment has moved at least temporarily to 29,000. In the last two years, Gettysburg has averaged about 1,925 students. Both institutions have increased enrollment around 5 percent above their target levels. They could easily reconsider earlier decisions that had not been forced upon them by events.

Third, colleges had flexibility in the utilization of their faculties. Given the larger environment of growth in higher education, an active labor market gave faculty members job mobility. Thus, although the number of faculty remained stable at an institution, its faculty was not so necessarily growing older and becoming increasingly inflexible in its assignments. Faculty specialists no longer needed at one place could go to some other place.

Fourth, the whole expanding system provided opportunities for many graduates. Students who wanted to be primary and secondary school teachers had jobs prospectively available. New Ph.D.'s could find jobs in other still enlarging institutions. There were opportunities within the whole system for women and members of minority groups without displacing someone else.

Fifth, income was growing. The sources of financial support, private and public, were solid, and the tuition gap between private and public institutions was somewhat more narrow than it is now. Operating funds, whose "historic" annual growth rate was about 2.5 percentage points per student above the rate of increase in the consumer price index, provided budget flexibility. Growth in income is at least as important, and perhaps more so, than growth in enrollment to institutional health.

In this context, an institution with an enrollment limit could function effectively in "high level steady state." From a relatively large number of applicants, it could select students whose course choices were well distributed over the range of existing programs and offer them a high-quality mix of programs because of the growth in operating funds. The active labor market for faculty meant that an individual institution could maintain a good age distribution with a fairly stable tenure ratio balance across departments. In a total faculty of stable size, there was a steady flow-through of new faculty infusing the institution with new ideas, vigor, and program mobility. With budget flexibility, some operating funds were available for innovative uses.

The planning and strategy required to operate within an enrollment ceiling meant that the institution had to identify its strengths and plan around them. When the plan was completed, the physical plant required little expansion, and sufficient funds were available to maintain it for the desired size.

Institutions like Gettysburg and Berkeley, it seems fair to say, are better off today than they would have been had they not set enrollment ceilings. By controlling growth under a plan, they were able to divert some of their energies toward developing internal flexibility and qualitative improvement. They could be somewhat more selective about their student body, and, although they are concerned about the possible future tenure ratios, officials at both institutions say that this is not a pressing problem now, and, with careful planning, the problem of increasing rigidity probably can be minimized.

The experience of these institutions explains why some past general descriptions of the benefits of steady state seem so at variance with the current facts—those benefits were the product of a favorable context.

Difficulties in Achieving Future Successes

If the current slowdown in growth were occurring because of thoughtful planning, its benefits would be more self-evident. If it were a gradual transition at a time of financial strength in higher education, under conditions of general economic growth, relative price stability, and optimism, enrollment stability might well be welcomed both for the achievement it represented, and the opportunities it created.

If access goals had been fully achieved, money freed by the decline in growth demands could be available for other uses.

Extended education programs could be strengthened. On campus, instruction could be enriched and more attention paid to the qualitative aspects of student life. New fields of study and research could be opened up. Colleges and universities could look inward, reassert their sense of purpose, and, after a period of being pulled in many directions by market and public policy forces, begin to reassert more control over the directions in which they were headed.

Planned, gradual slowdown amid general economic growth would mean that the labor market could absorb graduates. Persons doing advanced study would find that although academic career opportunities were declining, career opportunities in some other sectors of the economy would be increasing. In short, the gradual decline of enrollment growth in the context of continued economic growth might be welcomed as an opportunity to consolidate the long-term and recent gains of higher education and to reassert its creative capacity in the nation's service.

Today, however, most of higher education faces a declining rate of growth, not of its own planning, in a short period of time, in an unfavorable economic context, and (some believe) hard on the heels of two decades of underfinanced growth for some types of institutions. For many institutions, expansion in the "golden years" between 1958 and 1968 was, in part, financed by neglecting basic institutional needs such as institutional research and administrative support, and, more significantly, by mortgaging their futures—expansion was financed by debt. Buildings were erected without secure funds for their future operation and maintenance. Rather than an achievement or an opportunity for the creative use of funds, the decline in growth adds to the problems caused for these institutions by any already existing financial troubles facing academic institutions. Changes forced by suddenly reduced growth cannot be planned over a comfortable period.

Colleges and universities, also, are victims of serious inflation and of the policies used to fight it—as are their students. And no one claims that universal access is being fully funded.

But beyond all of these considerations lies the psychology

of the total context. The psychology of the growth years was one of expanding opportunity for individuals, even if some institutions were stable in size. Now that psychology is fundamentally changed. There are no expanding opportunities elsewhere to absorb the new teachers, the women and members of minority groups wanting to get in, the dissatisfied who want to move somewhere else, the unsatisfactory whom the institution wants to move elsewhere. Steady state for all is not at all like steady state for one. When no doors are open, a sense of claustrophobia sets in—and that is a morbid dread. All institutions are affected.

The early responses to reduced growth, then, are largely negative. They include the casualties of concentrating authority, rising students-to-faculty ratios, and reduction of quality in programs, students, and faculty capacity. The experience to date shows both how one man's anticipated heaven of steady state can be another man's actual hell of reduced circumstances or expectations, and also how close in time sequentially the old heaven and new hell can be. Higher education is in the throes of one of its greatest periods of transition. However productive and pleasant or destructive and painful the new state, once attained, may turn out to be, the processes of adjustment on campus are costly to tranquility and to quality alike.

How did this state of affairs arise?

3

Past Growth

The present is, in part, a product of the past. For higher education the past has been marked by remarkable periods of expansion.

Century of Growth: 1870-1970

Over the past century, the growth of higher education has been due both to deliberate educational policies and to the unplanned consequences of noneducational policies. In particular, the commitment in the most recent decades to mass access and the recognition, after World War II, that the creative capacity of colleges and universities represented a major source of national strength made growth a dominant characteristic of higher education.

By every relevant measure—students enrolled, campuses built, professors employed, degrees earned, or money spent— growth has been phenomenal. The percent of growth in student enrollments outstripped the percent of population growth by 34 times. This record was compiled despite periods of discouragement and even of open challenge. Over the past century, as in the 100 years before it, Americans provided generally strong support for higher education, but their support was periodically diluted by the effects of anti-intellectualism, political adversity, depression, student unrest, and war. However, in only four short periods—1917-18, 1933-34, 1943-44 and 1949-1951—was there an absolute decline in the number of students enrolled. During such declines, college and university officials were apprehensive about the future. Once these periods were over, however, colleges and universities again began to increase in size and number, and in their ability to respond to the complex demands of a growing nation. Eric Ashby noted this propensity to grow with the observation that "If the figures for resident degree credit enrollment since 1870 are plotted on a logarithmic scale, they fall on a straight line which, if continued, would envelop the whole 18-to-24 age group within a generation. Over the period 1870 to 1970 enrollments have doubled approximately every 14 to 15 years" (Ashby, 1971, p. 4).

After the mid-1950s, enrollments increased even more impressively—at the rate of almost 8 percent per year until 1970. At that rate, enrollment more than doubles in 10 years. The total number of students in degree-credit courses reached 3.6 million in 1960 and 7.9 million by 1970 (U.S. National Center for Educational Statistics, 1971b, p. 23; 1973b, p. 24).

Financial support grew even faster than enrollments. Total current income of institutions of higher education in 1940 was $715 million. Seventeen years later many institutions were enjoying record income years. Princeton University, for example, stated in a recent report that from 1957 to 1968 it "raised more money both for capital needs and current purposes than it had raised in its entire [212-year] history" (W. Bowen, 1972, p. 16). Those were the "golden years"—a single decade in which more money was spent on higher education than in all previous years since 1636. In 1959-60, the annual operating expenditures of colleges and universities were $7.6 billion. Ten years later they had increased to $24.9 billion. After 1970 this trend leveled off; had it continued, the annual operating expenditures of colleges and universities would have reached $51 billion (in 1970-71 dollars), or 3.3 percent of the GNP by 1980 (Carnegie Commission, 1972, p. 1).

The expansion of education in the United States was propelled primarily by three forces. One was the national commitment to expand access to higher education, a goal that was set more than a century ago and has become, in recent years, a dominant factor in public policy toward higher education. The second was the growing belief that the nation's welfare depends importantly on higher education, not only because expanded enrollment serves social justice and provides an educated citizenry, but also because a capacity for advanced study and research helps the nation meet important needs, some currently identified and others yet unknown. The nation's need for creative intellectual capacity, through centers of advanced study and research, is not directly related to the size of enrollments and has been financed in its own right. It also has been financed through enrollment growth, however, because, particularly at the state level, it has been easier for institutions to use numbers of new students as a rationale for seeking new funds than it was to make a separate case for increased funds to support advanced scholarship. A third force has been the increase of functions in the areas of service to agriculture, industry, and the professions; of student activities; of cultural programs for the community; and of adult education and other extension activities, among others.

A closer look at each of the first two forces for expansion reveals why each has been so important.

Extending access. For the last hundred years, more and more people in the United States have received more and more education. Opportunities for higher education, once available mainly to a narrowly based group of young persons, were opened to a wider segment of the population by the land-grant movement after the Civil War. A central theme of this populist movement was that through education persons in modest vocations could have higher status and greater productive ability: "If lawyers and doctors had higher institutions to serve them, farmers and mechanics should too" (Bowman, 1962, p. 526). The idea that what is worth doing for an elite is worth doing for others embodied the spirit of what Mary Jean Bowman described as "a roaringly optimistic and an almost frighteningly successful endeavor to create the men—and the women—for a mass economy" (ibid., p. 523). This philosophy, though not the only factor behind the rapid rise in enrollment, was a major one. In 1870, 52,000 undergraduate students were enrolled in the nation's colleges. Within a decade, enrollment doubled and, after another 50 years, by 1930, it had passed the one million mark (see Table 4).

Table 4. Undergraduate degree-credit enrollment, 1870-1970

	1870	1880	1890	1900	1910	1920	1930	1940	1950	1960	1970
Undergraduate students enrolled in degree-credit courses	(in thousands) 52	116	154	232	346	582	1,053	1,388	2,422	3,227	6,840
Percentage change		122	33	50	49	68	81	32	74	33	112
Percent of population aged 18 to 21	2.7	3.0	3.9	5.0	7.9	11.9	14.5	26.9	33.8	47.6

Source: Carnegie Commission on Higher Education (1971b, p. 127).

The GI Bill of 1944 opened up places in colleges and universities for 2.3 million veterans and was a major factor in further expanding mass access to higher education.

In the 1960s, access was still further extended, this time with efforts to achieve the ambitious goal of providing universal access, first for the college-age group and then for persons of all ages.

Table 4 presents the century-long record of this growing propensity of Americans to go to college. In only three of the last ten decades did enrollment rise by as little as one-third over the previous decade. In six of the decades, enrollment rose by 50 percent or more. Twice (in the 1870s and 1960s), it more than doubled in a decade.

While part of this enrollment growth was due to the growth of the college-age population, much of it was the result of an increased desire to attend college. Figures 3 and 4 show

Figure 3. Aggregate degree-credit undergraduate enrollment

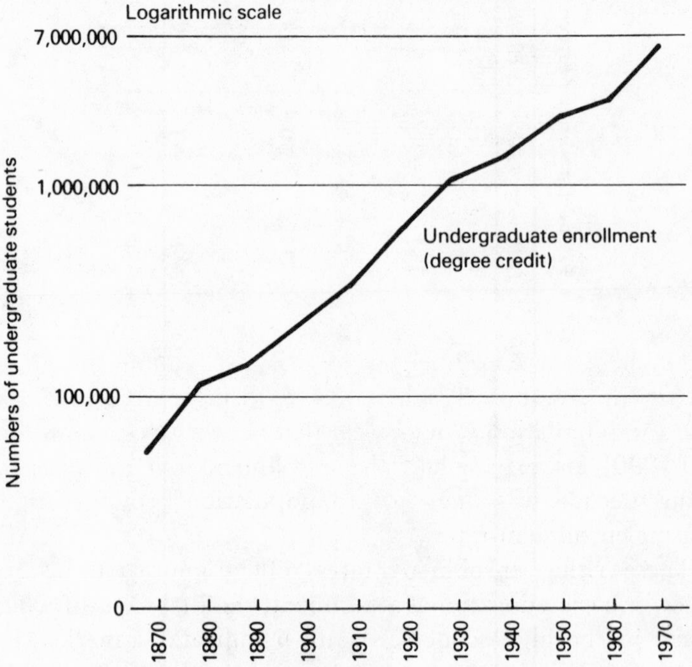

Source: Carnegie Council.

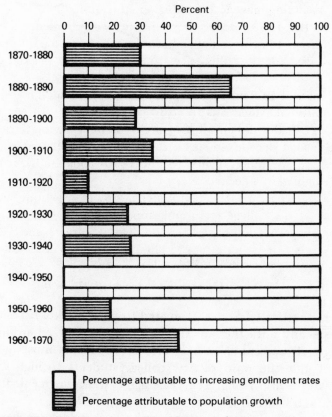

Figure 4. Percent of degree-credit undergraduate enrollment growth
attributable to population growth and enrollment rates

Source: Carnegie Commission on Higher Education (1971b, p. 127).

how much of the enrollment growth is attributable to population growth and how much is due to rising enrollment rates
within the population. They reveal that in every decade but one
(1880-1890) more than half the enrollment increase over the
previous decade was due, not to population growth, but to
increasing enrollment rates.

These rising enrollment rates reflect important historic
changes in basic educational attainment, the first signs of which
are seen in the high schools. Figure 5 indicates a marked improvement in the high school graduation rate after World War
II. At that time, fewer than 50 percent of the 17- to 18-year-

Figure 5. High school graduation rate 1946-1972

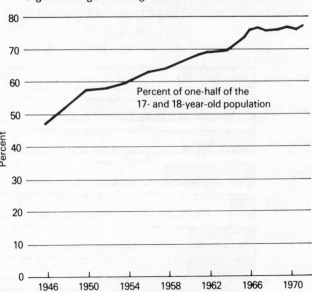

Source: U.S. Office of Management and Budget (1973, p. 76).

olds in the United States graduated from high school. That rate
rose steadily until the late 1960s, when it stabilized around its
present 78 percent. Not only are more students finishing high
school, but the ratio of new college students to high school
graduates is also rising. Ten years ago it was 50 percent. It now
stands at 58 percent.

These figures make clear not only that higher education
has been growing, but, more importantly, that the colleges and
universities are serving an ever-broadening segment of the American population—they are moving toward the broad policy goal
of universal access. Joseph Ben-David observed that socioeconomic status does have an effect on access to and success in
school, but in the United States this effect "is probably much
less than anywhere else in the world" (Ben-David, 1971, p. 3).
In 1960, racial minorities and women comprised 6.5 and 36 percent of enrollment, respectively. By 1970, these figures had
risen to 10.6 and 41 percent. As impressive as this record is,
universal access is far from being reached, and the rise in relative

enrollment of minority groups and low-income students has slowed down in recent years.

In retrospect, a turning point in college enrollment patterns was 1969, when enrollment rates of youthful males reached a peak and when enrollment rates of youthful women began to level off (Figure 6). More detailed data, not shown, indicate that enrollment rates of youthful black men and women continued to climb until 1972 and then fell back. (The enrollment rates of persons in the 22-to-34 age group in Figure 6 have been adjusted to eliminate postbaccalaureate students.) The data indicate that, for men in this age group, there has been little change in undergraduate degree-credit enrollment rates since 1969, although a fairly sharp increase occurred between 1960 and 1969. Among the women, there was a substantial increase from 1960 to 1969 and a modest increase in recent years.

It is important to consider the factors responsible for the recent decline in enrollment rates among those of traditional college age. Unfortunately, there are no good survey data that shed light on the relative importance of the various factors that have influenced this decline. At least four may be presumed to have played a significant role: (1) the abolition of the draft, (2) the sharply rising costs of college attendance that have been associated with accelerated inflation rates and accompanying increases in tuition and other college charges, (3) the changes that have occurred in the job market for college graduates, especially in the demand for schoolteachers and in the narrowing gap between wages received by high school and college graduates, and (4) liberalization of college rules to permit deferred admissions and "stopping out" of students in the midst of college careers. The fact that the sharpest contrast between the pronounced rise in enrollment rates in the 1960s and the decline since 1969 is found among youthful males suggests that the change in the draft situation is a major influence, but the other factors mentioned above have almost certainly played a significant role.[1]

[1] These trends will be discussed more fully in a forthcoming Council report presenting new enrollment projections. Conceivably, the rise in enrollment rates of youthful males between 1965 and 1969 could have been explained by withdrawals from the civilian noninstitutional population (the popula-

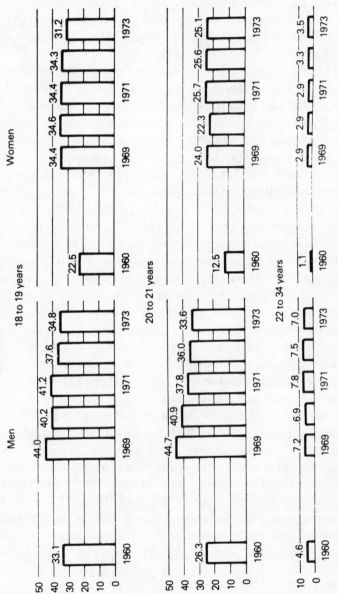

Figure 6. Estimated undergraduate degree-credit enrollment as percentage of population, by age and sex, 1960 and 1969-1973

Source: Adapted from U.S. Bureau of the Census data by the Carnegie Council.

As already noted, a further significant factor in explaining the failure of enrollment rates of college-age young people to increase in recent years has been a leveling-off of (and even a slight decline in) the high school graduation rate since the late 1960s.

Building creative capacity. The idea that the well-being of the nation depends importantly on higher education recurs through-out much of our history and is reflected in state and federal legislation supporting colleges and universities for activities ranging from agricultural research to training reserve army officers.

During World War II the importance of scientific activities at institutions of higher education to the national welfare was dramatically recognized when the Office of Scientific Research and Development decided not to set up its own research facilities, but, instead, to contract with universities (as well as with industry) for such activity. In 1945, Vannevar Bush, chairman of the office, reported to President Truman: "There should be a focal point within the Government for a concerted program of assisting scientific research conducted outside of Government." It should ". . . furnish the funds needed to support basic research in the colleges and universities, [and] should coordinate where possible research program on matters of utmost impor-

---

tion base for enrollment rates shown in Figure 6) as the number of young males in the armed forces increased. The decline in enrollment rates after 1969 could have been explained by increases in the civilian noninstitutional population as veterans returned. However, a special table presented by the Census Bureau in its 1972 report on school enrollment shows that, even when college enrollment rates are computed on the basis of the total population in each youthful male age group rather than on the basis of the civilian noninstitutional population, there is still a significant tendency for enrollment rates of young men to rise until 1969 and to decline thereafter (U.S. Bureau of the Census, 1974a, p. 3).

It should be added that, even if survey data were available on reasons for not going to college, they would probably not shed much light on the influence of the change in the draft situation, because many youthful males would not be likely to state that their decision not to enroll was attributable to the fact that there was no longer any need to enroll to escape the draft.

tance to the national welfare . . ." (Bush, 1945, p. 25). Five years later, the National Science Foundation he proposed was created, but, in the meantime, other agencies of government were doing what Bush had suggested.

A big impetus for federal support of education came on October 4, 1957, when the Soviet Union launched Sputnik. Official and public reaction in the U.S. was one of dismay over the apparent scientific lag in American schools and colleges. "Our schools are more important than our radar warning nets and more powerful than the energy of the atom," President Eisenhower told the nation in 1957. Out of this concern for the nation's intellectual development and strategic strength emerged the National Defense Education Act in 1958. It sought to strengthen the study of mathematics, sciences, and foreign languages; to identify and encourage able students; to improve research and experimentation; to bring about more effective utilization of television, radio, motion pictures, and related media; and to develop science information services. In 1963, Congress adopted the Higher Education Facilities Act to assist institutions to construct, rehabilitate or improve classrooms, laboratories and libraries.

The effects of these and other major legislative efforts were to make the federal government a highly important factor in the financing of higher education.

Until the 1970s, every president beginning with Eisenhower, in messages to the nation and to the Congress, linked the well-being of the nation to the contributions of higher education. That this message was heard less frequently in the early 1970s reflects the fact that reliance on the creative capacity of higher education was decreasing.

Problems of Growth

Not everyone was enthusiastic about the rapid growth of higher education and its expanded role. And rapid enrollment growth during the "golden years" was not evenly distributed. An analysis in *Science* magazine, by Jonathan A. Gallant and John W. Prothero (1972), revealed that in ". . . the fall of 1958, only ten campuses had total enrollments of more than 20,000 and these

accommodated eight percent of the national student population." One university campus with more than 30,000 students
enrolled 1 percent of the national total. By 1969, 65 campuses
had enrollments exceeding 20,000 and they accounted for 27
percent of all students. Twenty-six of these campuses had more
than 30,000 and accounted for 15 percent of the national
enrollment. In these campuses, the authors observed, "The
'community of scholars' has . . . undergone a radical transforma-
tion: in sheer size, the modern university resembles medieval
London rather than Oxford" (ibid., p. 38). The authors contend
that such growth in individual campuses is dysfunctional; that,
among other things, it produces administrative complexity,
bureaucracy, dead-end specialization, and alienation—costs that
outweigh expansion's alleged benefits of economy and scholarly
distinction.

In a larger analysis, Martin Trow (1973) shows how a clus-
ter of problems rather than individual problems are associated
with the transition from one phase of growth to another. The
transition from mass to universal access began to produce signs
of difficulty in the late 1960s. The labor market began to show
signs that it could not absorb all the college graduates as easily
as it could before. Student unrest was thought by some to be
related to the rapid growth and large size of colleges and universities. The government's reliance on higher education for mili-
tary-related research became an object of protest, as did the
cost of higher education to the nation.

But the problems of growth generally seemed smaller than
the benefits in the 1960s. On campuses and in legislatures
around the country, the hope and the expectation were that
growth would continue. Many legislators fought to establish
new campuses in their districts or to raise old ones to higher
status. Institutions and systems made optimistic growth plans.
As recently as 1970, many enrollment projections were for continued growth. Even in 1972, when the National Center for
Higher Education Management Systems used the Delphi method
to forecast important future developments in higher education,
its nationwide panel—students, legislators, citizens, faculty
members, and administrators—predicted the growing impor-

tance of management methods, but not that the management of declining growth and even of absolute decline would become a major problem (Huckfeldt, 1972).

Signs of a New Condition

Yet, for about the past four years, evidence has been accumulating that higher education is no longer a substantial growth segment of American society. The first symptom of the problem was financial. In 1970, studies indicated that the growth of institutional income was no longer keeping pace with expenditure growth. An enlarging cost-income gap in higher education was serious enough to be called a "new depression" (see Cheit, 1971). Then the impact of both a leveling and even reduction of enrollment rates and of demographic changes was identified. Office of Education reports revealed in 1972 that the rate of graduation from high school was leveling off. Later reports showed that a declining birthrate would further reduce the size of the pool of potential college students. Throughout this period, the labor market was no longer absorbing college graduates as readily as in the previous decade. By 1973, these facts, together with changes in the society in general, were beginning to affect the willingness of students to enroll. By 1973, it became apparent that the enrollment projections made in 1970 for the next decade were too high in every case.

Enrollment projections of both the Office of Education and the Carnegie Commission were high when compared to actual enrollment in 1971-72 to 1973-74, as Figure 7 shows. Both groups produced new enrollment projections, scaling down the estimated rate of growth in higher education.

The most recent official projections of the U.S. Office of Education (National Center for Educational Statistics, 1974b) are substantially lower than they were only a few years ago. The Office of Education now predicts that, for the remainder of this decade, the compound annual growth rate will not be 3.9 percent as predicted in 1970, but 1.3 percent. This would mean that by 1979 the number of degree-credit students would be 18 percent fewer than predicted by the Office of Education just four years ago—a reduction in predicted enrollment of almost 2 million students.

Figure 7. Comparison of Office of Education and
Carnegie Commission 1971 projections with actual
enrollments (in thousands)

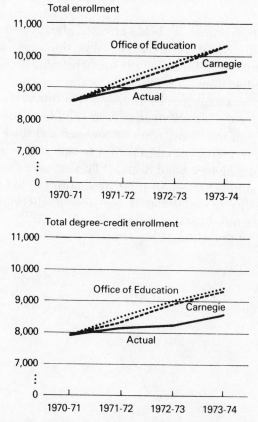

Sources: Haggstrom (1971, Table 1); "Opening Fall Enrollments,
1972 and 1973" (1974); U.S. National Center for Educational
Statistics (1972, p. 23); and U.S. National Center for Educational Statistics (1974b, p. 24).

Even if these new projections are too low, as may turn out
to be the case, it seems that for the remaining five years of this
decade an increasing number of institutions will be facing a
declining rate of enrollment (and, with few exceptions, income)
growth. If present trends are extended into the 1980s, the pressures posed by this new condition will become even more exacting. Then the task of a still larger proportion of colleges and

universities will be to operate with no enrollment growth, or as is possible, with decreasing enrollment. Not all institutions will be affected in the same way, but virtually all will be affected to some degree.

Some institutions are being affected already; even more are concerned for their futures. The direction and the rate of change in basic conditions are the overwhelming preoccupations of higher education. The fall from grace has come faster and harder than was expected by anyone just a few years ago. But is a declining rate of enrollment growth the likely course for the future? Or will the trend again be reversed and the historic rate of growth be reestablished? Or, is a totally different future in prospect—one of very rapid decline? Present uncertainty is great enough to stimulate each of these predictions. What predictions are now being made? What is our own prediction? To these questions we now turn our attention.

4

Enrollment Projections 1975-2000

Predicting future enrollments, as we have seen, is almost as hazardous as predicting the future of a college's endowment. Past projections on both have been less than perfect, and the uncertainties and sometimes conflicting trends in today's environment raise doubts as to whether any present projections will be any more reliable—or even *as* reliable. Some of the immediate signs are very mixed, their meanings so unclear that the *Chronicle of Higher Education* chose for its article on Fall 1974 enrollment trends the all-encompassing title, "Enrollments: Up, Down, and Hovering" (Magarrell, 1974). And, as we shall see, the future course of enrollment will be heavily affected by public policy, and public policy is still to be fully determined.

Clouded Crystal Ball

Current predictions for the longer-run future of higher education vary widely. On the one hand, the case has been made that higher education can and may enjoy continued, even dramatic, growth. Howard Bowen has noted that the service sector of the American economy is rapidly emerging as the dominant sector and that professional services are particularly responsible for this increase. Since higher education is a professional service of "high intrinsic value" and is also the main source of personnel providing other professional services, the growth of higher education should at least parallel the growth of the service sector of the U.S. economy. This argument for growth is bolstered by current enrollment trends (the increase in enrollment rates of 18- to 24-year-old women and of older adults of both sexes); the general predictions that people will have more leisure time, some of which would be used for further education; and the assumption that there will be no unforeseen needs for more highly skilled manpower. Howard Bowen writes:

> The limits of education are set, not by the dimensions of the jobs we see around us, but by the capacity of human beings to learn. And we are today far from reaching this capacity.

He concludes, with appropriate caveats, that:

> The higher educational industry might well double or triple in size during the balance of this century and a totally new kind of society might be created in which the level and the depth of education and the richness of culture would surpass that ever before achieved or even imagined (Bowen, 1974).

He sets this forth as a "possibility," not as a projection.

On the other hand, Joseph Froomkin shows in a recent analysis that college enrollments may decline because of "an excess of college graduates over the number of jobs for which college credentials are believed necessary" (Froomkin, 1974, p. 1). In projecting future enrollment levels, Froomkin describes what he calls three "scenarios."

In "Scenario 1: Continuation of the Status Quo," he projects to 1985 the continuation of the situation of the early 1970s, that is, undergraduate enrollments (including nondegree students) will remain relatively stable and the number of graduate students will increase between a quarter and a third. Froomkin adds that the levels of enrollment that result from his Scenario 1 are much too high in relation to the needs of the economy for college graduates.

Figure 8. How different projections and possibilities for enrollment in higher education compare with the 1974 level of enrollment (percentage comparisons)

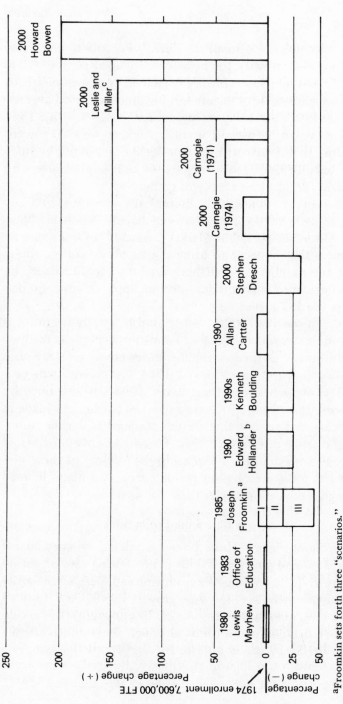

[a]Froomkin sets forth three "scenarios."

[b]Enrollment level for full-time undergraduates in the state of New York.

[c]Leslie and Miller assume that enrollment in higher education is linked directly to the rate of growth of the total gross national product. The Council has estimated the implied growth on the assumption that real GNP rises at an annual average rate of 3.5 percent a year from 1974 to 2000.

Sources: Appendix B.

In "Scenario 2: Small Decline," Froomkin notes the decline in the propensity for high school graduates to enroll in college. He assumes some further decline in degree enrollments, partly compensated by students seeking more technical degrees. If the trend to stay away from college continues, by 1985 enrollments in his Scenario 2 are likely to be at least 20 percent below those in Scenario 1. Even this decline would not be sufficient to balance the supply of jobs for college graduates with the demand for jobs (the supply of graduates).

The most pessimistic of Froomkin's scenarios, and the most pessimistic of the projections included here, is his "Scenario 3: Floor Set by Labor Market Demand." In this scenario, he estimates that in order to bring the supply of college graduates and the number of available jobs into overall balance by 1985, college enrollments would decline approximately 50 percent from the 1974 level.

Thus, in the year 2000, there could be nearly six times as many students enrolled in higher education according to Bowen's "possibility" as there would be under Froomkin's Scenario 3 (assuming that the conditions of 1985 continued to the year 2000). The range between these two extremes is well filled by other predictions. Figure 8 shows a series of predictions made in recent years and reveals that serious students of higher education see sharply differing futures. (A comparative analysis of these predictions appears as Appendix B).[1] Some of these predictions are, for quite obvious reasons, more warmly welcomed within higher education circles than are others.

Carnegie Base-Line Projections

Our projections suggest three phases of change in enrollments between now and the year 2000: (1) a slowing rate of enrollment growth; (2) a leveling of enrollment and, perhaps, an absolute decline; and finally, (3) slow growth again. These Council estimates anticipate a slower rate of declining growth than do most other detailed projections, although the Council predictions can hardly be called bullish. By the early 1980s, we fore-

---

[1] For another analysis of enrollment estimates see Mangelson et al. (1974).

Figure 9. Total enrollment in higher education, actual 1973 and projected 1980-2000, Carnegie Council base-line compared with projections assuming constant 1973 enrollment rates, total and full-time equivalent

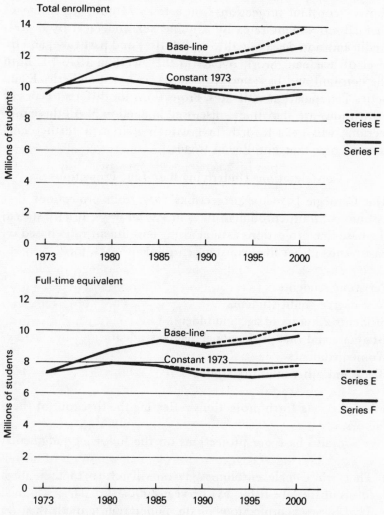

Note: Series E uses population estimates from census Series E data, which assume a fertility rate of 2.1. Series F uses population estimates from census Series F data, which assume a fertility rate of 1.8.

Source: Carnegie Council.

see a leveling of total enrollment that would last until about 1995.[2] After 1995, the Council predicts very slow growth in enrollments. Figure 9 shows these aggregate national enrollments for higher education projected to the year 2000. It also shows "constant projections" on a 1973-74 basis which means that all enrollment rates by age and sex and race, by degree-credit and non-degree-credit, by full-time and part-time, and by level of academic work remain as they were in 1973-74. Both the constant and base-line projections are based on Series E and Series F population estimates. Projections for different types of institutions are shown and discussed in Section 5. All these projections will be set forth in greater detail in a forthcoming Council report on enrollment trends.

Considerations Underlying Base-Line Projections

The Carnegie base-line projections vary from projections that assume constant enrollment rates in several ways. Briefly stated, the base-line projections assume rising enrollment rates based on past trends rather than constant enrollment rates, for:

Part-time students
Non-degree-credit students
Students 22 years of age and older
Graduate and first professional degree students
Women students
Black and other minority students

Figure 10 sets forth projections reflecting the first four of these factors.

We also base our projections on the following judgments:

• That white male enrollment rates will return to their peak levels of the late 1960s by the year 2000.
• That Series F projections of the population may prove to be

---

[2] In our figures and tables, which present data for five-year intervals, it appears that the leveling off begins after 1985, but more detailed data show that the leveling off actually begins after 1982.

Figure 10. Headcount enrollments by level and type, 1960-1973, and projected 1973-2000 (in thousands)

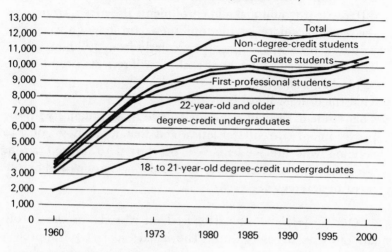

Source: Estimated by Carnegie Council.

Table 5. Headcount enrollments by level and type, 1960-2000 (numbers in thousands)

Year	Degree-credit undergraduates		Graduates	First profes-sionals	Non-degree-credit	Total
	18-21	*Other*				
1960	1,911	1,220	356	96	206	3,789
1970	4,071	2,779	900	170	661	8,581
1973	4,459	2,990	989	219	1,007	9,664
1980	5,138	3,293	1,050	258	1,813	11,513
1985	4,952	3,613	1,148	295	2,129	12,137
1990	4,717	3,522	1,072	287	2,220	11,818
1995	4,905	3,701	1,120	299	2,154	12,179
2000	5,355	3,844	1,182	311	2,102	12,794

Source: Carnegie Council.

reasonably reliable. We note, in particular, that the birthrate is still falling. However, we also show in Figure 9 the overall difference it would make in enrollments if Series E were to be the more accurate prediction; then enrollment projections would be somewhat higher, particularly from 1990 on.
- That the demand for schoolteachers will reflect current pupil-to-teacher ratios.
- That the draft will not be reinstated.
- That student aid will continue to rise in accordance with the provisions of current legislation and that funds now going to veterans who are students will be shifted to nonveterans as Vietnam War veterans move into older age groups and enroll-ment of veterans declines.

Our projections also are based on a study of the enroll-ment rates of all age groups. The usual "lock-step" approach begins by estimating the future number of high school graduates and thus is tied directly to the future number of 17- to 18-year-olds, while the "all age groups" approach allows for differing future rates of change in the numbers of older adults (see Appendix C).

Our projections, of course, are no better than our assump-tions and judgments, and we are highly conscious of the many unknowns.

Uncertainties

Any projection of enrollment must recognize that there are ex-traordinary uncertainties in the future of higher education.

(1) Foremost among these is the state of the economy it-self. At the present time, it is even more difficult than usual to forecast the behavior of the American economy. There have been significant fluctuations in price levels, unemployment, gross national product, and disposable personal income. The base-line enrollment projections in this section assume that the economy will behave somewhat as it has in the past but with a somewhat higher rate of inflation and a somewhat lower rate of growth in the real GNP; that inflation will not accelerate

rapidly and the GNP not decelerate rapidly. We consider that these projections are consistent with an economy where the consumer price index will increase at an annual rate of about 4 to 6 percent and the real national product will grow at an annual rate of about 3.5 percent.

(2) Even with reasonable price stability and economic growth, labor market changes could have great direct effects on enrollments. Enrollment rates could also be significantly affected by declining rates of return on investment in a college education. We have assumed, however, that enrollment rates will not be sharply influenced by labor market developments.

(3) Possible changes in life-styles of the young, and their effects, if any, on higher education are little easier to predict today than they were 15 years ago, when no one predicted the pronounced changes of the 1960s and early 1970s.

(4) The same may be said about the impact of a volunteer army. It is likely to be older than an army staffed by the draft, but the effects, if any, on enrollment cannot be predicted.

(5) Changes in the high school graduation rate would have immediate consequences for college enrollment rates. We assume no sharp changes. Such changes have not been easily predictable in the past.

(6) The same uncertainty applies to the birthrate itself. An increase, which we do not assume, would, within five years, have an effect on demand for teachers, and even before that might have a positive effect on enrollment rates for those wishing to become teachers.

(7) Veterans benefits now being paid under the GI Bill will begin to decline shortly. The extent of the decline is not easy to predict, but we believe the funds no longer expended on veterans benefits should be used for general student aid, as we recommend later in this commentary.

(8) Graduate enrollments are particularly volatile. The job prospects for new Ph.D.'s at their level of training and in their fields of specialization are generally the most negative in history. At the same time, interest in law and medicine has skyrocketed. Some young persons may decide not to enter graduate work because of lack of good job prospects after they get

their degrees. Others may attend because of lack of current job prospects and thus for lack of anything else to do. Since so many graduate programs are oriented toward specific occupations and occupational prospects change so much, the internal distribution of graduate students, as well as their total volume, is likely to be in constant flux. We note that first-time graduate enrollment rose by 7.6 percent from fall 1973 to fall 1974 even as the prospects for most degree recipients became more problematical.

(9) Colleges will seek to tap the following new pools of potential students: the pool of high school seniors (currently 3 million on an annual basis), the pool of high school graduates who are now nonattenders (1.5 million on an annual basis), the pool of college dropouts (750,000 on an annual basis), the pool of potential transfer students from two-year colleges, and the pool of adults. But their success is as yet uncertain.

(10) The major uncertainty, however, is public policy. Just as the GI Bill transformed higher education after World War II, public policy could once again alter the course of enrollments. The effects for higher education of possible changes in public policy toward student aid, institutional aid, graduate education, and research are probably more important than all the other uncertainties combined. In the base-line projections, we have assumed no major shifts in policy, but subsequently we urge (Section 7) that such changes be made. The changes we suggest would significantly alter the projections in this section. Public policy, federal and state together, can affect any enrollment projections, our own included, in the range of at least 10 percent in either direction, both up and down; and this creates a potential "zone of uncertainty" of 20 percent or more in totality. Withdrawal of present support, on the one hand, and a substantially increased support on the other, can make at least this much difference. Higher education is a heavily subsidized segment of society and thus highly sensitive to public actions. Public policy also affects the rate of inflation and the degree of economic growth, and they, in turn, both affect the course of higher education. Higher education is not an autonomous element in society; it is, rather, a subsystem, albeit with an unusual

degree of independence. Nevertheless, higher education is highly affected both by direct public policy and by the general performance of the economy (for a discussion of the great impact of inflation, as an illustration, see Harris, 1970).

Assumptions, judgments, uncertainties—these are the stuff of which projections are made. It takes a dash of bravado to make a projection; but it shows a touch of madness to believe too much in its invincibility. We offer our projection as one possible guide to the murky future, knowing that it is only one guide among several that are being offered—and quite various they are, as we have seen at the start of this section. The best advice to consumers of any of these projections, ours included, is: *caveat emptor.*

We now turn to a discussion of enrollment prospects for types of individual institutions related to the base-line projections set forth in this section. It should be remembered, of course, that our base-line projections set forth higher rates of enrollment than do the constant projections. If the constant projections should prove more accurate, then all types of institutions would be affected, but to different degrees, in a negative direction in their enrollment levels.

5

Forecasts for Institutions: A Diversity of Outlooks

National enrollment projections estimate the trends of enrollment figures of over 2,800 institutions. When these total enrollment figures are broken down by institutional category, such as two-year colleges, liberal arts colleges, comprehensive colleges and universities, and research universities, it becomes apparent that the overall projection comprises a great variety of movements. Colleges and universities in some categories stand above the overall trend, while others stand below it. Even when the total enrollment trend is at a no-growth level, as is predicted for the late 1980s, some types of institutions (public two-year colleges, for example) may be growing and others (such as the less highly selective liberal arts colleges) might be declining.

Importance of the Institution

This dynamism makes projecting enrollments by institutional categories even more hazardous than projecting total enrollments. But if important changes occur in response to the new conditions of higher education, it is within individual colleges and universities that the impact will be felt. Thus it is important to know as much as possible about the internal dynamic quality of the evolving enrollment patterns. Given the national enrollment projections, what can be forecast for institutions? What factors influence the enrollment outlook for different categories of institutions? What adjustments can institutions make to shape their enrollment outlook?

We will examine these questions for six main groups of institutions: (1) *universities* (all doctoral-granting institutions); (2) *comprehensive colleges and universities* (all institutions that offer a liberal arts program as well as several other programs, including graduate and professional, but no—or extremely limited—doctoral programs); (3) *highly selective liberal arts colleges* [as defined by Astin's (1971) selectivity index, or ranked as a leading baccalaureate-granting institution by the National Academy of Sciences]; (4) *less highly selective liberal arts colleges* (all liberal arts colleges that do not meet the criteria of "highly selective"); (5) *public two-year colleges* (all two-year publicly controlled institutions); and (6) *private two-year colleges* (privately controlled two-year colleges and institutes).

Independent professional schools and other specialized institutions are not included. (Readers interested in the complete definitions of these categories and the names of institutions under each should consult *A Classification of Institutions of Higher Education,* Carnegie Commission on Higher Education, 1973a).

In 1973, the most recent year for which complete data are available, a total of 7.1 million students (FTE basis) were enrolled in institutions of higher education. This figure is distributed among the six groups of institutions in these percentages:

Universities	33.4
Comprehensive colleges and universities	33.1
Highly selective liberal arts colleges	2.7
Less highly selective liberal arts colleges	6.9
Public community colleges	22.5
Private two-year colleges	1.4

Source: Carnegie Council calculations based on unpublished NCES data on opening fall enrollment, 1973.

As we saw in Section 4, Carnegie base-line projections are for slow growth until about 1985. The forecast for 1985 to about 1995 is for essentially no growth. Then there will be slow growth to the end of the century.

What may the enrollments be in 1985 for the different categories of institutions? The discussion that follows is based (1) on the Carnegie base-line projection and (2) on FTE-student counts. We approach answers to the question as follows:

First, suppose each category kept its current (1973) share of students—and many institutions will be fighting to hold this "share of the market."

Second, suppose the changing trends in shares of the period 1963 to 1973 were to continue (and they were substantial) —and many institutions are looking, either with fear or with hope, at the developments of the past decade as one signal about the future.

Third, suppose a look were taken at only the past few years (1968-1973)—and they were years of dramatic, even searing, developments for higher education, still fresh in mind.

Fourth, suppose four of the most important factors now at work were to continue their differential influences—and the four we have selected are each quite significant individually and, in total, can make quite a difference.

Fifth, suppose the ability of individual institutions to make selective adjustments were evaluated—and each institution finds itself with its own individual environment and history and internal characteristics.

Sixth, suppose judgments were applied in adding up the consequences of each of the five earlier "supposes"—and it is recognized that the judgments of others may vary greatly from our own.

We face a most intricate series of possibilities. There is no agreed-upon map of the future. Yet the prospective shape of the future, however uncertain, can greatly affect how institutions and individuals act today and tomorrow. Thus we try to look at the future from six different points of view for whatever interest and help this may be to others.

Forecast 1: Status Quo of Shares

The simplest, though perhaps least credible, assumption about future enrollments is that institutional shares will not change. Table 6 shows how a projected 8,971,000 FTE enrollments for 1985 would be distributed among categories of institutions if each category retained its 1973 share of FTE enrollment.[1]

From the institutional point of view, Table 6 presents a fairly satisfying picture of the future: slow but steady growth for all types of institutions. If the number of institutions did not change, for example, the average university of 1973 (14,400 students) would gain more than 3,800 FTE students by 1985. Proportionately similar gains would be made by each institutional group, as the last two columns in the table show. But this scenario will never be acted out.

Forecast 2: Share Trends of 1963-1973

Since the distribution of enrollment among categories of institutions was not stable in the 10 years preceding 1973, there is little reason to assume that it will be unchanging in the future. A more trustworthy prediction might be gained by extrapolating FTE-enrollment distribution trends for each of the institutional categories. Table 7 shows the projected FTE enrollment for 1985 divided among the six groups of institutions, assuming

---

[1] Figure 9 in Section 4 shows the base-line projection for total FTE enrollments as follows:

	Series E	Series F
1980	8,865,000	8,865,000
1985	9,345,000	9,345,000
1990	9,169,000	9,100,000
1995	9,536,000	9,378,000
2000	10,435,000	9,673,000

These projections in Section 4 include the FTE enrollments for all institutional categories analyzed in this section, plus a category not considered in this section, "Professional Schools and Other Specialized Institutions." The FTE-enrollment projection for 1985 used in this section (Section 5) excludes "Professional Schools and Other Specialized Institutions," and therefore is 8,971,000. We excluded this one category because we do not include it in our analysis.

Table 6. Projection of 1985 FTE-enrollment levels for six institutional categories assuming each category retains its 1973 share of FTE enrollment

	1	2	3	4	5	6	7
	Number of institutions (1973)	Actual FTE enrollment (1973)	Percent share of FTE enrollment	Projected FTE enrollment (1985)[a]	Net additional FTE students (1985) (4−2)	Average size of institutions (1973) (2÷1)	Average number additional FTE students per institution (1985) (5÷1)
Universities (campuses)	165	2,372,000	33.4	2,996,000	624,000	14,400	3,800
Comprehensive colleges and universities	469	2,355,000	33.1	2,970,000	615,000	5,000	1,300
Highly selective liberal arts colleges	141	193,000	2.7	242,000	49,000	1,400	300
Less highly selective liberal arts colleges	541	491,000	6.9	619,000	128,000	900	200

	1	2	3	4	5	6	7
	Number of institutions (1973)	Actual FTE enrollment (1973)	Percent share of FTE enrollment	Projected FTE enrollment (1985)[a]	Net additional FTE students (1985) (4−2)	Average size of institutions (1973) (2÷1)	Average number additional FTE students per institution (1985) (5÷1)
Public community colleges	841	1,599,000	22.5	2,018,000	419,000	1,900	500
Private two-year colleges	224	102,000	1.4	126,000	24,000	500	100
TOTAL	2,381[b]	7,112,000	100.0	8,971,000	1,859,000	3,000	800

[a]Columns 4, 5, and 7 assume (1) that 1985 FTE enrollment will reach the level projected in the Carnegie baseline projection; (2) that each institutional classification will retain the same percentage of FTE enrollment that it had in 1973; and (3) that the number of institutions will remain the same as in 1973.

[b]Excludes "Professional Schools and Other Specialized Institutions."

Sources: 1973 figures are calculations by the Carnegie Council based on unpublished data from the U.S. Office of Education, National Center for Educational Statistics. Projections are by Carnegie Council.

Table 7. Projection of FTE-enrollment levels for six institutional categories assuming for each that the percent of change in FTE-enrollment-share trend of 1963-1973 continues to 1985

	1	2	3		4	5	6	
	Actual FTE enrollment (1973)	Projected FTE enrollment (1985)[a]	Percent share of FTE enrollment		Net additional FTE students gain (loss) (1985)	Average size of institutions (1973)	Average number of new FTE students in 1985:	
			(1973)	(1985)			Based on 1963-1973 trend[b]	Based on 1973 relative share[c]
Universities (campuses)	2,372,000	1,857,000	33.4	20.7	(515,000)	14,400	(3,100)	3,800
Comprehensive colleges and universities	2,355,000	2,942,000	33.1	32.8	587,000	5,000	1,300	1,300
Highly selective liberal arts colleges	193,000	135,000	2.7	1.5	(58,000)	1,400	(400)	300
Less highly selective liberal arts colleges	491,000	323,000	6.9	3.6	(168,000)	900	(300)	200

| | 1 | 2 | 3 | | 4 | 5 | 6 | |
| | | | Percent share of FTE enrollment | | | | Average number of new FTE students in 1985: gain (loss) | |
	Actual FTE enrollment (1973)	Projected FTE enrollment (1985)[a]	(1973)	(1985)	Net additional FTE students gain (loss) (1985)	Average size of institutions (1973)	Based on 1963-1973 trend[b]	Based on 1973 relative share[c]
Public community colleges	1,599,000	3,642,000	22.5	40.6	2,043,000	1,900	2,400	500
Private two-year colleges	102,000	72,000	1.4	0.8	(30,000)	500	(100)	100
TOTAL	7,112,000	8,971,000	100.0	100.0	1,859,000	3,000	800	800

[a]Assuming that 1963-1973 percent of change in share of FTE students enrolling in each classification continues from 1973 to 1985 and that in 1985 professional schools and technical institutes (excluded from calculations) will continue to retain their 1973 share of FTE enrollment.

[b]Column 4 divided by number of institutions in each classification. It is assumed that the number of institutions will not change between 1973 and 1985.

[c]From Column 7, Table 6.

Sources: 1973 figures are calculations by the Carnegie Council based on unpublished data from the U.S. Office of Education, National Center for Educational Statistics. Projections are by Carnegie Council.

that the percent of change in their FTE-enrollment-share trend will continue in the same way as in the past decade.

Table 7 presents a vastly different view of the future from the constant share view of Table 6. Instead of steady growth in all categories, only the public community colleges gain a larger share of enrollment. One category—the comprehensive colleges and universities—holds relatively constant, while the other four decline. In all four cases, the decline is significant and, in the case of private two-year colleges, it is severe. By 1985, private two-year colleges have but 0.8 percent of FTE enrollment. The less highly selective liberal arts colleges would suffer only a slightly less serious decline. Their 1973 share of FTE enrollment, a substantial 6.9 percent, drops to 3.6 percent. Universities lose about one-third of their 1973 share of FTE enrollment. The average university campus, using this basis for forecasting, would drop from 14,400 FTE students to about 11,300. Highly selective liberal arts colleges would register a significant loss. Their share of FTE enrollment would drop from 2.7 percent to 1.5 percent. In contrast, the public community colleges would more than double, their average size rising from almost 2,000 to almost 4,300 FTE students.[2] The most striking characteristic of Table 7 is its contrast with the results produced by the stable share forecast of Table 6. What accounts for these differences?

The difference between these two enrollment forecasts measures the importance of enrollment shifts in the decade between 1963 and 1973. The great growth of public community colleges occurred during the 1960s, when the total number of institutions more than doubled, reaching 805 in 1970.[3] Total degree-credit enrollment rose from 400,000 to over 1.5 million.

---

[2]The number of community colleges can, of course, be expected to grow. If their average size remained at the 1973 figure of 1,901 FTE students, the number of institutions under this projection would grow from its present 916 (including two-year branches of four-year institutions) to 1,969.

[3]The total number of public two-year colleges in 1970 is based on the Carnegie Commission classification, which includes two-year branch campuses of multicampus systems that are not included separately in U.S. Office of Education data.

In that period, as a related factor, because of a sharp rise in interest in non-degree-credit courses, many more students enrolled in the public two-year colleges. Other categories of institutions benefited from this rise in student demand, but not nearly to the same degree. During that decade more students came to many campuses for part-time degree-credit study, but, when the numbers are totaled, the public two-year colleges gained the most. These institutions also gained students as a result of the decisions of some universities and highly selective liberal arts colleges to limit their enrollment growth in the 1960s. In contrast, the total number of private two-year institutions declined in this decade by 5 percent. The private two-year colleges were adversely affected by the growing number of public institutions.

The declining demand for teachers probably had some adverse effect on all institutions, but its main enrollment effects were felt by the less highly selective liberal arts colleges, the universities, and the comprehensive colleges and universities.

Overall, the big changes were the rise of the public community colleges and the beginning of the fall in teacher education —and about 20 percent of higher education has historically been directed to teacher education. Teacher education now accounts for only about 10 percent of enrollments. When such a massive change takes place in such a large component, the reverberations can be severe. They not only affect total institutions but their component parts, particularly schools of education and divisions of humanities.

This was a very special decade and thus projections based on it are not likely to be produced on the stage of history. In particular, the rise of the community college movement was a one-time phenomenon.

Forecast 3: Share Trends of 1968-1973

Since the number and magnitude of factors causing these enrollment shifts were anything but uniform between 1963 and 1973, the effects of more recent changes might be given even greater emphasis with a forecast based on the last five years rather than on the entire 10-year period.

Table 8 presents such a forecast, dividing projected FTE enrollment for 1985 by shares derived by a linear extrapolation of the percent of change in the enrollment share trend for each of the institutional categories from 1968 to 1973.

The consequences of projecting from the more recent changes are most favorable for universities, comprehensive colleges, and both categories of liberal arts colleges. All would have larger shares under the five-year base projection than under the 10-year projection. In contrast, the enrollment share of public community colleges would increase only slightly, and that of private two-year colleges would decline somewhat. Both would have smaller shares of enrollment under the five-year base projection than under the 10-year projection. The public community colleges would have 25 percent of FTE enrollment, a drop from the nearly 41 percent projected on a 10-year base. Enrollment in the private two-year institutions would decline to 0.5 percent of total FTE students.

Thus we see that projecting from the more recent base period would put universities, comprehensive colleges, and liberal arts colleges in a slightly better position in 1985 than when the full decade of shifts is projected. How does the latter half of the decade between 1963 and 1973 differ from the first five years?

Two important trends established in 1963-1968 were modified in the period 1968-1973. First, the rapid rise in the number of students in part-time study, both degree-credit and non-degree-credit, was absorbed primarily in the public two-year institutions from 1963 to 1968. It would appear that the other categories of institutions were competing somewhat more effectively for these students from 1968 to 1973.

The second important shift concerns undergraduate full-time students. In the first half of the decade, this group shifted away from universities, liberal arts colleges, and, to a lesser extent, comprehensive colleges and toward public two-year institutions. In the second half of the decade, universities, comprehensive colleges and universities, and highly selective liberal arts colleges began to regain a larger share of this student group, especially women. Consequently, when these two changes,

Table 8. Projection of 1985 FTE-enrollment levels for six institutional categories assuming for each that the percent of change in FTE-enrollment-share trend of 1968-1973 continues to 1985

	1	2	3		4	5	6		
			Percent share of FTE enrollment		Net new FTE students gain (loss)	Average size of institutions	Average number of new FTE students in 1985: gain (loss)		
	Actual FTE enrollment (1973)	Projected FTE enrollment (1985)[a]	(1973)	(1985)	(1985)	(1973)	Based on 1968-1973 trend[b]	Based on 1963-1973 trend[c]	Based on 1973 relative share[d]
Universities (campuses)	2,372,000	2,888,000	33.4	32.2	516,000	14,400	3,100	(3,100)	3,800
Comprehensive colleges and universities	2,355,000	2,996,000	33.1	33.4	641,000	5,000	1,400	1,300	1,300
Highly selective liberal arts colleges	193,000	341,000	2.7	3.8	148,000	1,400	1,000	(400)	300
Less highly selective liberal arts colleges	491,000	440,000	6.9	4.9	(51,000)	900	(100)	(300)	200

(continued on next page)

Table 8 (*continued*)

	1	2	3		4	5	6		
			Percent share of FTE enrollment				Average number of new FTE students in 1985: gain (loss)		
	Actual FTE enrollment (1973)	Projected FTE enrollment (1985)[a]	(1973)	(1985)	Net new FTE students gain (loss) (1985)	Average size of institutions (1973)	Based on 1968-1973 trend[b]	Based on 1963-1973 trend[c]	Based on 1973 relative share[d]
Public community colleges	1,599,000	2,261,000	22.5	25.2	662,000	1,900	800	2,400	500
Private two-year colleges	102,000	45,000	1.4	0.5	(57,000)	500	(300)	(100)	100
TOTAL	7,112,000	8,971,000	100.0	100.0	1,859,000	3,000	800	800	800

[a]Assuming that 1968-1973 percent of change in share of FTE students enrolling in each classification continues from 1973 to 1985 and that in 1985 professional schools and technical institutes (excluded from calculations) will continue to retain their 1973 share of FTE enrollment.

[b]Column 4 divided by number of institutions in each classification. It is assumed that the number of institutions in each classification will not change between 1973 and 1985.

[c]From Column 6, Table 7.

[d]From Column 7, Table 6.

Sources: 1973 figures are calculations of Carnegie Council based on unpublished data from the U.S. Office of Education, National Center for Educational Statistics. Projections by Carnegie Council.

together with other facts affecting enrollment shares, are projected from 1968, the relative position of universities, comprehensive colleges and universities, and highly selective liberal arts colleges changes in a favorable direction.

In general, universities and highly selective liberal arts colleges are in a particularly favorable position to meet competitive pressures by modifying admission standards. But all types of institutions can make adjustments and counteradjustments, almost indefinitely. It may also be noted that the comprehensive colleges and universities became more comprehensive during this most recent period and less concentrated on teacher education; and that the less selective liberal arts colleges were more vulnerable than the highly selective liberal arts colleges to both the increasing competition from public comprehensive colleges and universities and to the decline in the demand for teachers.

First Conclusions from Institutional Forecasts

An analysis of the results of these forecasts produces several preliminary conclusions about forecasting for institutions:

(1) The division of enrollment shares among categories will keep on changing, although probably not as dramatically as over the past decade.

(2) The ability of institutional categories to make adjustments in response to new situations, new opportunities, new competitive pressures is substantial. And these adjustments are made after a time-lag only sufficient to provide an opportunity for an institution to perceive the new situation; to assess responses to it; and to get the necessary concurrences and resources to take action. The time-lag is shorter than one might expect given the reputation of higher education for moving slowly and only under extreme pressure. But some categories are in a better position to respond to certain new situations than are others.

(3) Major new developments can take place quite unexpectedly and, perhaps, are hardly recognized when they first occur, like the dramatic rise of the community college movement. What may the next ones be? Videocassettes? Self-paced instruction?

(4) What happens in society at large can have great impacts inside higher education, like the fall of the birthrate and the quick subsequent decline in the demand for teachers.

(5) Student choices are an important influence as, for example, in the rise in part-time study.

(6) Public policy, as in the creation of community colleges, is a major force at work on the comparative rise and fall of categories of institutions.

These preliminary conclusions suggest that one potentially helpful method of forecasting for institutions is to try to identify factors that are likely to influence future enrollments among different categories of institutions, and then to consider how these factors, and the ability of institutions to adjust to them, might affect future enrollment shares.

Forecast 4: Four Factors That May Affect
Future Enrollment Shares

Factors which may influence future enrollment shares of different categories of institutions are likely to include, it now seems, the continuing effects of population changes, the market for teachers, increased interest in part-time non-degree-credit study, and public policy toward support of private institutions.

Population changes will have two general effects. First, since there will be relatively fewer 18- to 21-year-olds, as Figure 11 shows, institutions of different types will find themselves in increased competition for this source of undergraduate students. Those institutions most highly dependent on this pool of students are likely to be most affected.

A second effect of population change is, of course, a declining demand for teachers. As we noted earlier, the most immediate effects are being felt at the elementary and secondary school levels, and by the institutions which train teachers for these levels. The slowing of enrollment growth has also reduced the growth in demand for college teachers. Table 9 shows the actual demand for additional teachers for three recent years (1968, 1970, and 1972) and projections through 1982 under current policies.

Offsetting these adverse effects on enrollment of popula-

Figure 11. Actual and projected size of the 18- to 21-year-old
population (total and as percentage of population over 15)

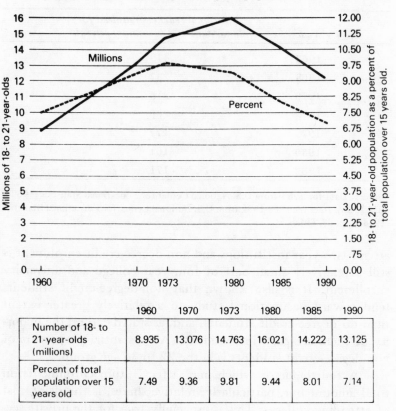

	1960	1970	1973	1980	1985	1990
Number of 18- to 21-year-olds (millions)	8.935	13.076	14.763	16.021	14.222	13.125
Percent of total population over 15 years old	7.49	9.36	9.81	9.44	8.01	7.14

Sources: U.S. Bureau of the Census (1971a; 1972c).

tion changes are the increased numbers of part-time students of
all ages. The increased interest in part-time study, particularly
non-degree-credit study, which is mostly part-time, is a major
phenomenon of recent years which, as Table 10 indicates, is
likely to continue. Part-time degree-credit study will grow
slightly faster than full-time study; and non-degree-credit study
will continue to grow substantially relative to full-time degree-
credit study.

Remarkably few facts are known about these non-degree-
credit students. We do know that, for the most part, they

Table 9. National demand for additional teachers as projected
by the Office of Education (thousands)

Year	Additional teachers required for elementary and secondary schools
1963	419
1968	237
1970	215
1972	206
1975	177
1980	161
1982	171

Sources: Data for 1963 from U.S. National Center for Educational Statistics (1969b, pp. 51, 53). Data for 1968-1982 from U.S. National Center for Educational Statistics (1974b, pp. 67, 69).

attend two-year institutions and non-degree-credit enrollment is still a relatively small part of four-year college and university enrollment. It is also known that non-degree-credit students tend toward occupational study to a relatively greater extent than do degree-credit students, and, as stated earlier, the majority of them are part-time students. A substantial proportion of non-degree-credit students is in the 22 to 34 age group.

A fourth factor which may affect future enrollments, in total amount but, particularly, relative shares, is the rising cost of attending colleges. This is especially true for the private sector, where the tuition differential with public institutions has been growing. A public policy most likely to affect enrollment shares in the future is the growing state interest in solving this financial difficulty.

Historically, public funds played an important part in the establishment and expansion of "private" institutions. Most of the original nine colonial colleges, for example, were supported, in part, with public money. Until recently, however, the states receded in importance as a source of funds for private institutions. That trend has been sharply reversed in recent years in many states, as the financial problems of private institutions grew and as the states became concerned both with the future

Table 10. Actual and projected degree-credit, full-time and part-time, and non-degree-credit enrollment in higher education (1963-2000)

| Year | Degree-credit enrollment (thousands) | | | | Non-degree-credit (thousands) | Total enrollment | Percent non-degree-credit |
	Full-time	Part-time	Total (1)+(2)	Percent part-time (2)÷(3)			
1963 (actual)	3,068	1,426	4,494	32	271	4,765	6
1968 (actual)	4,937	1,991	6,928	29	585	7,513	8
1973 (actual)	5,894	2,763	8,657	32	1,007	9,664	10
1980	6,790	2,910	9,700	30	1,813	11,513	16
1985	6,805	3,203	10,008	32	2,129	12,137	18
1990	6,431	3,167	9,598	33	2,220	11,818	19
1995	6,514	3,511	10,025	33	2,154	12,179	18
2000	7,271	3,421	10,692	32	2,102	12,794	16

Source: Data to 1973 are from the U.S. National Center for Educational Statistics (1973b). Projections are by Carnegie Council.

of the private sector and the diversity of higher education. Thus many of the states have begun various forms of assistance to private institutions, the most important of which is financial assistance to students. Table 11 shows how rapidly this form of state support grew in the two-year period 1972-73 to 1974-75.

Table 11. Rising state support for student financial aid programs:
1972-73 to 1974-75 (in millions)

School year	Total dollars	Dollars to private institutions[a]	Dollar increase to private institutions	Percentage increase in dollars to private institutions
1972-73	315.5	189.3	–	–
1973-74	364.2	218.5	29.2	15.4
1974-75	456.9	274.1	55.6	25.4
Increase 1972-73 to 1974-75			84.8	44.8

[a]Assumes 60 percent of state aid to student financial programs goes to private institutions. See The National Commission on Financing Postsecondary Education (1973, p. 97).

Source: Survey by Joseph D. Boyd, cited in Winkler (1974, p. 1).

The National Commission on the Financing of Postsecondary Education found a growing number of programs benefiting private institutions, including tuition equalization grants (in at least nine states) and general institutional support (in nine states). The State Student Incentive Grant program initiated by the federal government in 1973-74 will, no doubt, accelerate the development of state programs. The National Commission found that nearly every state legislature was considering some new program proposal and concluded: "There is particularly strong interest now in many states in increasing aid to private institutions" (National Commission on the Financing of Postsecondary Education, 1973, p. 101).

Table 12 shows how, in our judgment, these selected factors are likely to affect enrollment shares in the different categories of institutions.

Table 12. Estimated effects of four selected external factors on the share of enrollments held by six types of institutions

Institutional type	Fewer 18- to 21-year-olds	Declining market for teachers	More part-time[a] students of all ages	Rising state support for private higher education	Total consequences for enrollment shares in 1985 compared to 1973
Universities	Average	Worse than average	Worse than average	Average	Smaller
Comprehensive colleges and universities	Average	Worse than average	Average	Worse than average	Smaller
Highly selective liberal arts colleges	Worse than average	Average	Worse than average	Better than average	Same
Less highly selective liberal arts colleges	Worse than average	Worse than average	Worse than average	Better than average	Smaller
Public community colleges	Better than average	Better than average	Better than average	Worse than average	Larger
Private two-year colleges	Worse than average	Average	Worse than average	Better than average	Smaller

[a]Includes both degree-credit and non-degree credit.

The overall impact of these four selected factors on relative enrollment shares is highly uneven. For the first three—fewer 18- to 21-year-olds, a declining market for teachers, and more part-time students of all ages—only the public community colleges are predicted to experience a "better than average" impact on their enrollment share. The others have either an "average" impact, or "worse than average" impact. The decline in demand for university and college level teachers has, of course, a particularly pronounced impact on universities. In the case of the fourth factor—rising state support for private higher education—enrollment shares would fare "better than average" in highly selective liberal arts colleges, less highly selective liberal arts colleges, and private two-year colleges. Public community colleges and comprehensive colleges and universities (most of which are public) would be relatively worse off. The private comprehensive colleges would, of course, be better off, as would the private universities.

The summary of these judgments, as shown in the final column of Table 12, is that the effect on the 1985 enrollment shares of these four factors would be to reduce them for universities, comprehensive colleges, less highly selective liberal arts colleges, and private two-year colleges. Community colleges would enlarge their enrollment share, while the share of enrollment held by the highly selective liberal arts colleges would remain about the same. These estimated changes in shares should in each case be related to the "status quo" projections, set forth earlier, which reflect 1973 shares.

But we have seen earlier that, after a lag, enrollment share trends are modified partly because some "losing" institutions are able to make adjustments which make them more attractive to students. What affects the ability of institutions to make these selective adjustments? How may this ability be distributed among institutional categories?

Forecast 5: Ability to Make Selective Adjustments

The enrollment shifts cited earlier for 1963 to 1973 suggest that selective adjustments are being made in response to enrollment shifts. The ability to make such adjustments appears to be influenced, in considerable part, by several factors, some within the control of an individual institution, some not. Enrollment is, of course, not the only index of future health. The availability of adjustments affects all aspects of institutional welfare.

(1) Size. Boulding (1974) concludes, tentatively, that larger organizations seem better able to manage decline than smaller ones. Other things being equal, larger organizations enjoy more budgetary flexibility, more room to maneuver, and they often have greater influence on state policy. Thus multi-campus systems have more room for maneuver than do single-campus institutions. While it is true that smaller organizations can mobilize total effort more readily, they cannot make cuts in their operations and programs with as little overall damage as can larger organizations. This is because their effort is more unitary and less a composite of relatively unrelated parts, selected ones of which can be severed with little effect on others. Moreover, the ability to bring resources to bear on management problems—to gather data and provide analysis, for example—is often a function of size. Universities and comprehensive colleges should benefit most from this factor. Also, larger institutions are more likely to be in a situation in which cost per student will not change very much with overall changes in enrollments and thus they can move moderately in either direction without great impacts. But smaller institutions are more likely to be operating on a sloping cost curve and any movement downward in enrollment moves them up the curve of per student costs and may have great impacts on them.

(2) Urban location. The newly enlarged demand for part-time study is primarily an urban phenomenon. Urban areas offer many such opportunities and have better public transportation. Thus urban private colleges can compete effectively in this market with public residential institutions, but appear to be having difficulty competing with public community colleges. Cities also seem relatively more attractive to full-time students than has historically been the situation. Universities, comprehensive colleges, and public community colleges, should, on balance, benefit most from the operation of this factor, since more of them are in urban locations.

(3) Competitive status. For private institutions, competitive status is determined partly by tuition differentials with public institutions, and partly by the number of such public institutions within close proximity. Public institutions face competition from other public institutions, of course, including, most recently, the increasingly active vocational-technical institutions. No one category of institution is shielded from competition, but, on balance, it appears that public community colleges, highly selective liberal arts colleges, and universities are, as general categories, less likely to be buffeted by competitive pressures than are the institutions in the other categories.

(4) Reputation. Drawing power is created by special characteristics that may range from strong religious ties to a good record in employment placement, from a good climate to a good academic program. It would seem to be a function of clear institutional identity, and its measure is the ability of institutions to withstand competition. Clearly some institutions in all categories have great drawing power. If any categories have more than an average share, they would appear to be the highly selective liberal arts colleges and the universities; and that portion of the less highly selective liberal arts colleges with strong religious and community ties.

(5) Age. Emerging institutions lack the advantages of institutions long in operation. Established institutions have an alumni base, and necessary plant, management experience and credibility with funding sources. These and other advantages of a mature organization can, of course, be offset by the encumbrances of age. Tradition can be a barrier to prompt response. On balance, however, it would seem that older is better, and the comprehensive colleges and public community colleges probably benefit least from this factor.

(6) Decisions of 1960s. The growth decisions of the 1960s may be a heavy burden in the next decade for those institutions that moved too far and too late into graduate work, research, and teacher training, with the accompanying capital decisions. Some private institutions in all categories are burdened by decisions to grow that were made in the 1950s and 1960s, often in response to government urging. They incurred substantial debt and planned buildings without secured funds for future mainte-

nance and operation, or realistic plans for debt service. No category of institutions has a corner on the bad effects of these decisions. The great public pressures put on institutions in the 1960s implied continuity of support for expansion and induced decisions about enrollments and research which, in retrospect, seem less than wise. Among the categories of institutions least burdened by such decisions in the 1960s are the two-year institutions and the highly selective liberal arts colleges. Those institutions that moved too far and too late toward a heavy concentration on research and graduate studies may be the most burdened, and they are found particularly among the universities and the comprehensive colleges and universities.

(7) Graduate enrollments. Specialization, a necessary condition of advanced graduate study, is also a source of serious adjustment problems at times of enrollment shifts. Universities are especially vulnerable to this problem. Thus, the recent shift in emphasis away from doctoral work in the humanities and in physics has left some university departments with highly trained specialists and far less demand for their services. The adverse effects of these shifts on universities are only partially offset by the rising interest in professional and master's level study. The comprehensive colleges and universities are the main beneficiaries of revived interest in occupational study at the master's level. Almost all of the graduate degrees granted by these institutions are at the master's level. The volatility of graduate enrollments most affects the universities and comprehensive colleges.

(8) Health professions. Institutions with established programs at all levels in the health professions, from practical nurses to medical scientists, are particularly well situated for enrollments for the near future. However, enrollment in these fields has been rising so rapidly that shortages may be overcome before long. Already, shortages of nurses have begun to disappear in large urban areas.

(9) Financial condition. Highly selective liberal arts colleges, universities, and comprehensive colleges, and, to a lesser degree, public two-year institutions, are probably best able to find the resources needed to make selective adjustments.

(10) Management and attitudes toward reality. Even

though little is known about the management of declining rates of growth, the ability to learn will depend on a willingness to face facts, to share information, and to be accountable to those who provide support. These qualities and the good management practices they foster can be found in institutions in all categories. Public community colleges, however, not only still have substantial growth prospects but also their sense of realism and their sensitivity to external changes contrast sharply with that demonstrated by many institutions in other categories.

Although these 10 illustrative factors relate to categories of institutions, they relate much more precisely to the situations of individual institutions. Thus, they constitute primarily a check list for institutions in evaluating their futures; but they also have an impact on the shares of enrollment among categories through their impact on single institutions.

Table 13. General capacity of six types of institutions to make selective adjustments to new conditions in higher education and to respond to competitive pressures

	Universities	Comprehensive colleges and universities	Highly selective liberal arts colleges and universities	Less highly selective liberal arts colleges	Public community colleges	Private two-year colleges	Total number of institutions (1973)[a]	Percent of all institutions (1973)	Percent of FTE enrollment (1973)
Above average	X				X		1,006	42	56
Average		X	X				375	16	20
Below average		X[b]		X		X	1,000	42	24

[a]Table excludes professional schools and technical institutes.

[b]Comprehensive colleges and universities are rated both "average" and "below average." To calculate number of institutions and percentages, the number of these institutions and their enrollments were divided evenly between these two classifications.

These judgments are summarized in Table 13. That summary indicates that two categories of institutions—universities and public community colleges—are likely to have a better than average capacity for selective adjustments and for response to competition. Private two-year colleges and the less highly selective liberal arts colleges are, perhaps, generally in a below average position. Comprehensive colleges and universities may find themselves in either an average or below average position and highly selective liberal arts colleges in an average position; the private comprehensive colleges are particularly likely to be in the below average situation.

About 40 percent of the institutions (with 56 percent of the total enrollment) are estimated to have a better than average capacity for selective adjustments and for resistance to competitive pressures, and an equal proportion (with about 24 percent of the total enrollment) to have a below average capacity to respond to the changes and constraints facing them.

Forecast 6: Comprehensive View

From the preceding analyses, we conclude that, although the enrollment share of universities is likely to be reduced by external factors, they have an above average capacity to make individual, selective adjustments and to withstand competition. Public community colleges appear to benefit from the external forces and to have the capacity to adjust to them. The less highly selective liberal arts colleges, the private two-year colleges, and, to a lesser extent, the comprehensive colleges, face both external pressures toward reduced enrollment shares, and factors which make their capacity for selective responses often below average. A significant segment of each of these three categories is comprised of institutions that are Catholic in origin, and this leads to a special concern for the welfare of this whole group of institutions. They do, however, because of their special relationships with many secondary schools, have the opportunity to offer integrated secondary and higher programs at a saving to students that is not possible where the separation between secondary and postsecondary institutions is much more distinct. The highly selective liberal arts colleges appear to be in a position to hold their own, because of both external factors and ability to respond.

We thus end up with two broad categories of institutions: (1) those institutions which, on the average, are likely to do relatively well with their enrollments and institutional health—the public community colleges, the universities and the more highly selective liberal arts colleges; and (2) those institutions which, on the average, are likely to do relatively less well, given the same amount of effort, with their enrollments and institutional health—the comprehensive colleges and universities (particularly the private ones), the less highly selective liberal arts colleges and the two-year private colleges. The phrase "the same amount of effort" is very important. Doing "relatively well" or "relatively less well" depends, of course, on what the average condition turns out to be, and we have suggested it will be slower growth, then no growth and then slow growth.

But these judgments too, must be modified, for the enrollment fate of institutions will be shaped by additional considerations. There are many exceptions to the general rules.

Pluralistic Variations

In the Berkeley Center Survey (see Appendix A) responses from certain types of institutions seemed more optimistic than warranted by the projected condition of the overall categories into which they fell. Council and Berkeley Center staff members visited and telephoned a number of these institutions and the findings from these inquiries tell much about the variety and the sources of strength of individual educational institutions. Most of all, they show that even when overall trends are firmly established, some specific kinds of institutions are not likely to be affected by them. The basic health of these institutions is conditioned by factors peculiar to their own situations.

The additional inquiries produced evidence that suggests that several factors common (1) to black colleges, (2) to women's colleges, and (3) to some religiously-affiliated (mainly fundamentalist) institutions are working to produce more optimism about the future of these particular kinds of institutions than the aggregated data would seem to warrant for the broader categories into which they have been grouped above. A number of private two-year colleges fall into one or more of these three specialized situations and appear to have greater hope for the future than recent and current overall trends might suggest. Among the factors that create opportunities for these institutions, the following four stand out:

(1) Many institutions report new strength from their special link to a particular constituency—a religious or sex group, an ethnic or racial group. The special, focused characteristics of these institutions are not a limitation, but apparently a source of vitality. Although none has escaped the serious problems of inflation, the tuition gap, and a continuing cost-income squeeze, many report new support from the interest and efforts of their special constituents. These advantages range from additional financial help from church or denomination to new student interest because of special ties to the type of institution. In short, supportive involvement is growing for institutions with specialized constituencies.

(2) Special vigor is related to a clear statement of mission. Institutions that have formulated their missions and can communicate them effectively in program statements are benefited.

(3) There is often clear evidence of new, vigorous leadership. That leadership is revealed not only in successful efforts at mission-clarification and at curricular and building efforts, but also in recruitment, in fund-raising, and in closer links to institutional constituencies.

(4) Viewed in the longer term, many of these institutions are not favored by recent history. They were forced, early on, to learn survival skills, to plan. They did not grow rapidly or even at all during the "golden years." Now they are operating from a low base and actually enjoying small increments of growth, rather than working to cope with the deceleration effects of a reduced rate of growth. Most of these institutions are private institutions, but a few are public black institutions, which are being helped by gaining financial parity with the other public institutions in their states. Black colleges, both public and private, have also gained from federal aid to low-income students and to "developing institutions."

The United States is a pluralistic nation, not a monolithic

one. When there are general difficulties, many institutions and individuals can fall back on their origins, on the special groups or missions that caused their creation, on their specialized, rather than generalized, appeal and sources of support. So it is for a number of institutions of higher education, seemingly passed by in the course of general events but rescued by their identification with one or more of the varied forces that together help constitute the overall society—in plurality there is strength.

Importance of Location

The judgments about capacity of institutions to adjust to new conditions must be further modified to reflect enrollment shifts as a function of geographic location. Table 14 shows the importance of location in the total enrollment experience of the four years between 1970 and 1974. Nineteen states had above average growth, the remaining 32 (including the District of Columbia) had below average growth, with 3 states—Montana, North Dakota, and South Dakota—showing an absolute decline.

Table 14. Percentage changes in total state enrollment compared with change in total national enrollment (1970-1974)

State	Percentage change		
	Total	*Public*	*Private*
Above average growth			
Nevada	81.2	81.2	76.3
South Carolina	64.6	93.8	3.1
Alaska	49.1	51.8	23.7
Virginia	41.5	51.0	0.8
Arizona	38.9	37.1	120.3
Alabama	38.7	44.8	5.6
Florida	30.8	36.7	6.6
North Carolina	29.8	40.1	3.4
Rhode Island	29.5	21.4	39.6
Vermont	27.4	32.3	21.0
New Jersey	26.9	42.3	(4.7)

Table 14

| State | Percentage change | | |
	Total	Public	Private
Above average growth (continued)			
Maryland	24.7	28.9	8.3
Texas	24.1	28.3	3.9
Georgia	23.0	24.9	15.2
California	21.7	22.6	14.0
Tennessee	21.3	25.5	9.9
Oklahoma	20.6	22.1	12.9
Hawaii	20.0	22.5	(2.9)
New York	18.4	27.9	6.3
Below average positive growth			
Illinois	17.9	26.0	(0.6)
Mississippi	17.5	19.3	4.6
New Hampshire	17.0	23.1	9.7
Louisiana	16.4	18.4	6.4
Connecticut	16.2	24.2	4.8
Massachusetts	15.5	30.0	6.5
Michigan	15.2	16.9	4.7
Delaware	15.0	18.0	(0.4)
Kentucky	14.9	22.1	(11.2)
Washington	14.4	14.2	16.2
New Mexico	14.0	13.5	18.7
Oregon	13.4	14.4	5.7
West Virginia	12.8	18.9	(13.6)
Wisconsin	12.5	15.9	(6.1)
Colorado	10.6	13.4	(9.7)
Kansas	10.5	14.4	(13.8)
Missouri	9.1	7.5	13.5
Arkansas	8.9	7.8	14.8
Pennsylvania	8.7	15.1	0.3
Ohio	8.5	9.8	4.8
Maine	7.3	9.0	2.4

(continued on next page)

Table 14 *(continued)*

State	Percentage change		
	Total	*Public*	*Private*
Below average positive growth (continued)			
Wyoming	6.0	6.0	—
District of Columbia	5.5	17.9	3.2
Indiana	5.2	9.7	(5.8)
Iowa	4.4	11.7	(7.8)
Utah	3.8	10.6	(6.8)
Minnesota	3.4	1.8	10.3
Idaho	3.3	5.4	(4.1)
Nebraska	0.6	5.0	(14.0)
Decline			
Montana	(6.9)	(7.6)	(0.7)
North Dakota	(9.4)	(11.2)	33.5
South Dakota	(12.4)	(13.7)	(7.6)

Note: Total national enrollment grew 18.1 percent from 1970 to 1974. Enrollment in public and private sectors grew 22.7 percent and 4.4 percent respectively over the same period.

Sources: 1974 figures from "Opening Fall Enrollments, 1972, 1973, and 1974" (1974); 1970 figures from U.S. National Center for Educational Statistics (1971a, pp. 16, 22, 28).

Among the states that grew faster than the national average, almost half were in the South. California and New York—the two largest states—were also among those with above average growth.

Midwestern and northeastern states are prominent among those with less than average growth. The three states with absolute declines in enrollment are clustered in the Northern Plains and Mountain States.

Summary

Before turning to a consideration of institutional effort, it may be of value to summarize our earlier suggestions that, in terms of shares of total enrollment, it is better to:

- Attract all ages rather than only 18- to 21-year-olds
- Provide for part-time rather than only full-time students
- Be less, rather than more, dependent on teacher education
- Have public state support than not
- Be of an effective size rather than forgo the economies of scale
- Be located in an urban rather than in a rural location
- Have comparatively low tuition and few local competitors rather than high tuition and many local competitors
- Have a national reputation or a devoted specialized constituency rather than neither
- Be older rather than younger as an institution
- To have made wise expansion commitments in the 1960s rather than to have become overcommitted
- Have a stabilized undergraduate enrollment rather than a volatile graduate enrollment
- Be related to the health professions rather than not
- Be in a sound financial condition rather than not
- Be closely related to reality rather than not
- Be located in the South or California or New York rather than in other parts of the country and particularly than in the North Plains and Mountain States

These and other factors will help determine to be or not to be. That question, once again, draws a complex answer.

"The muddled state," as Henry James once noted (in *What Maisie Knew*), is often "one of the very sharpest of realities" and "has color, form and character." There is at least as much to be learned from a disaggregated approach to the future of higher education as from the more usual, and also more simplistic, aggregative approach.

But, at the end of these considerations, the issue of what individual institutions may do to affect their own futures remains unsolved.

6

What Institutions Can Do

Higher education in its entirety faces slower growth and then the prospect of essentially no growth. The potential impacts on some types of institutions and some individual institutions, as we have seen, will be greater than for others. Many institutions will face decline in all or at least a portion of their efforts and what Kenneth Boulding has called the "management of decline" is no easy task:

> Perhaps the crucial problem [for higher education] is that the problems of administration become more difficult and the quality of administrators is apt to decline as the more able ones find more attractive opportunities in the expanding sectors.

He adds that:

> Many [management] skills which were highly desirable and which were selected in the last thirty years may no longer be the skills which are needed in the next thirty years. . . . Yet we know so little about decline that we are not even sure what these [needed] skills are (Boulding, 1974).

Some institutions will face overall decline or major change

of status, not just declining or slow growth. The Berkeley Center Survey asked college administrators the question: "Looking ahead to the next five years, is the character of your institution likely to undergo any radical change, such as merger, consolidation or closure?" Written comments on the question add the possibility of "public take-over" for some private institutions as an additional "radical change." A sobering 10.6 percent of all responses are "yes," even though the greatest impact of the declining rates of enrollment growth does not come until the mid-1980s. These affirmative answers are, quite naturally, unevenly distributed by type of institution. According to the survey responses, public institutions are slightly more likely to see radical change than private institutions. The expectation of radical change, however, is most concentrated among private liberal arts colleges which are less highly selective and private two-year colleges. Looking ahead to 1985, this overall 10.6 percent figure appears generally reasonable.

Table 15. Expectation of "radical change" in institution over next five years (percentages)

| *Categories of institutions* | *Control of institution* | |
	Public	*Private*
Universities	7	0
Comprehensive Colleges and Universities	11	4
Public Liberal Arts	12	
Private Liberal Arts I		5
Private Liberal Arts II		15
Two-Year	12	13
Total	11	10
Total Public and Private	10.6	

Note: "Radical change" includes merger, consolidation, or closure, and also, for private institutions, a transfer to public status.

Source: Berkeley Center Survey.

Some institutions will be under much greater pressures than others, but most will be under some pressures to adapt to the new conditions. If and when effective adjustments are made to the new condition of American higher education, it will have been, in large part, through the efforts of individual institutions, not an abstraction called "higher education." The needed adjustments will move higher education beyond the problems of declining growth and the end of growth. Some colleges and universities will not survive. Others—perhaps new types of institutions without current prototypes—will come into existence. But basically, coping with the problems of declining growth and then reaching a more stable but still dynamic position will fall to existing institutions that will continue to exist.

In the short run, these efforts will be made under present public policies. In the section to follow, however, we recommend public policy changes whose effects would be to produce enrollment growth above that of the base-line projections in Section 4. In our judgment, both the institutional efforts discussed in this section and the public policy changes set forth in the next are essential.

In this section we discuss the institutional actions we believe to be necessary, whether or not public policy is revised. Among these institutional efforts are the analysis and strategic planning needed to attain flexibility in operations and program offerings; more sophisticated cost-cutting and management; a measure of institutional specialization; and new methods of operating in increasingly competitive markets. The discussion in this section assumes the short-term outlook for all institutions to be one of leveling enrollment growth and of increasing competition for students and funds within present public policies. We discuss, first, some considerations affecting many, if not most, institutions, and then turn to developments by type of institution.

We wish to stress in advance the need for institutions to act on their own behalf: (1) public policy may not develop as favorably as we recommend; (2) even if it does so, there will be some delay; (3) in any event, the prospective enrollments may be at lower levels—even considerably lower levels—than we project; (4) even under favorable public policy and enrollment results, most institutions will still be under some pressures; (5) institutions have an obligation to do their best to adapt to the new circumstances and not to place the burden on public authorities alone to bail them out—in fact, good faith institutional effort is a prior requirement for favorable public response; and (6) in the course of competition, some actions are desirable as a basis for success, even if not needed for institutional survival, and should be undertaken as a matter of course regardless of changes in the external environment.

Strategy: Analysis of Situation and Planned Flexibility

Those institutions facing declining growth, or no growth, or actual decline may profit from developing, if they have not already done so, an overall strategy for the new condition, one which projects, realistically, several years into the future.

An overall strategy can be formulated only after a careful analysis of the college's (or system's) condition, one which directly questions generally accepted (but often not precisely formulated or heretofore tested) wisdom about the environment of the college (or system), its strengths, weaknesses, and role. A good place to start is with the recognition that growth fosters neither the habits of mind nor the organizational arrangements required for adjusting to declining growth. Thus since 1970, when it was first understood that a "new depression" was overtaking higher education, many colleges and universities have modified their tactical goals of increasing income and increasing enrollment to include the goal of cutting costs. Colleges and universities have, in varying degrees, joined the new management movement, adopting new systems approaches, but more important, employing older management methods with increased vigor. Many institutions have had considerable success in holding down their expenditure growth, finding new sources of funds, and going from buying to selling in the student market.

What they may now need to do is to advance these various tactical efforts to the next stage—the development of an overall institutional (or system) strategy based on a realistic understanding of the new situation. Past growth or academic plans, those of say 10 or even 5 years ago, are valuable sources of information for this process. They should be examined for assumptions, if any, which are patently invalid now, but which are still being used in the planning and operation of the institution.

One example common in private institutions is the assumption that deficits can be projected into future planning on the premise that they can be eliminated by future income growth. The security of private institutions requires a new kind of forward financial planning. The type of planning ..ow in use in some private institutions [Stanford University (1974) is one example], which brings together hard estimates of income, enrollment and costs, and bases institutional academic plans on a projected equilibrium between costs and income, is now required.

An example of an unrealistic assumption used in planning by some public institutions is the premise that they are immune to the dangers of closure or consolidation of program.

Government officials at all levels are inclined to believe that the planning and forms of accountability in higher education are too often unrealistic, unconcerned with the needs of the larger society, and not representative of the true position in which institutions find themselves. Institutions, both individually and within associations, should work to improve the measures by which they would want public agencies to judge institutional performance. The preliminary statement on university benefits and performance developed by the University of Washington is an excellent example of an approach to the important issue of accountability (Committee on Educational Benefits/Performance Measures, 1974). We believe that representatives of government will be receptive to institutionally developed measures of accountability if they are credible, not self-serving.

It is always difficult to face the future realistically, and doubly so at a time of declining growth. Some of the responses to the Berkeley Center Survey are more optimistic, in the judgment of Center staff members, than either recent history or current trends would seem to warrant (Glenny et al., 1975). This situation poses a special challenge to academic leadership. If administrators and faculty leaders are to inform their institutions about their futures and to work to create a climate receptive to planning and change, they must give this leadership task special attention. Some of the factors and considerations set forth in Section 5 might serve as one partial basis for the analysis of institutional prospects.

Recommendation 1: *That institutional leaders prepare analyses of their institutions to determine, as accurately as possible, the present situation and the factors shaping the future course. These analyses should be used to inform their colleagues and constituents, and should be part of a larger effort designed to create attitudes receptive to and conditions conducive to change.*

The problem of inflexibility is a major concern to nearly all institutions and systems. Reduction in income growth has already forced cuts and attention to budgeting practices which diminish internal sources of flexibility. A Council staff survey of 10 institutions in a no-growth status asked what annual portion of the operating budget should consist of flexible funds in order to achieve program objectives. The answers range from 1 to 3 percent. None of the 10 institutions have this necessary measure of flexibility, and one had no budgetary source of flexibility at all.

Reallocation is the main source of flexibility when income growth ends. Some state systems (Wisconsin is a good example) have modified their funding formula to help campuses affected by sudden enrollment declines. But reallocation under no-growth raises issues of centralized planning and authority which are little understood, and sometimes feared. Economist and author Robert Heilbroner is pessimistic about loss of freedom as a correlate of no growth in the economy as a whole (Heilbroner, 1974). The fact is, we have not yet devised the institutional means of reallocation in a democratic state.

Reallocation puts great stress on procedural arrangements. Internally, colleges and universities are generally not well suited for the type of decision-making it requires. They developed in a decentralized form and are not organized to express the overall objectives of the campus. Although decentralized forms of

governance can be highly effective in growth, in decline they
are more likely to paralyze the organization than help to
define it.

Successful reallocation must involve peer review and participation, and this is most onerous to accomplish. Judgments
to determine which programs should remain and which should
lose out are very difficult to make. In most situations, individual academic programs are seen either as complements to each
other or as independent. Few are viewed as substitutes which
afford easy "close-neighbor" choices.[1]

Experience shows that, even in cases of a program which
by all relevant criteria should be phased out, a faculty with all
the necessary information, procedures, and guidelines is likely
to find it very difficult to make a clear or prompt decision.
Historically the tested criteria have applied to what to add and
not to what to subtract—and criteria for the latter are more
rigorous.

The Berkeley Center Survey reveals the increased interest
administrators have in using reallocation for institutional
change. Figure 12 shows that, in all categories of institutions
(except private two-year colleges), administrators expect to add
fewer new programs between 1974 and 1980 than they did
between 1968 and 1974. Figure 13 shows that these administrators will be placing much greater emphasis on program review
as a means for institutional change. Despite the difficulties
noted earlier, administrators expect that institutional change
will come more from program substitution than from program
addition.

Institutions are beginning to try to make this reallocation
process a way of life. Between 1968 and 1974 only 6 percent of
all institutional administrators in the Berkeley Center Survey
made "extensive" use of course elimination or consolidation to
free resources for reallocation. For the next six-year period,
three times as many report they expect to make "extensive" use

---

[1] For a cogent analysis of the difficulty of comparing academic programs
see Balderston (1974, Chapter 3, pp. 38-73).

Figure 12. "Increase" in the number of instructional programs (undergraduate level)—actual 1968-1974 as compared with projected 1974-1980

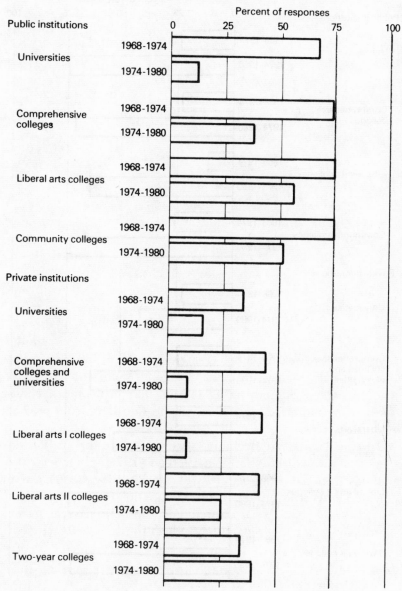

Source: Berkeley Center Survey.

Figure 13. "Extensive" use of program evaluation (all levels)—actual 1968-1974 as compared with projected 1974-1980

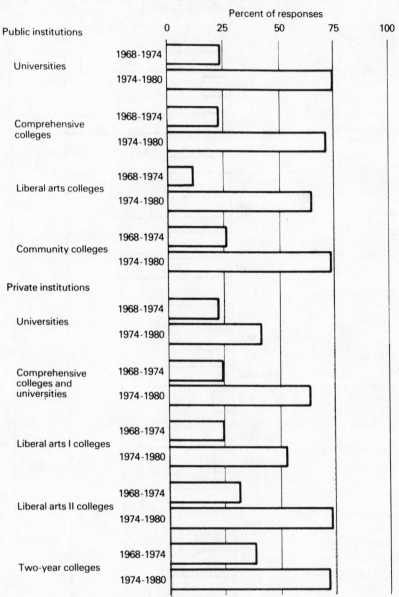

Source: Berkeley Center Survey.

of that practice for reallocation.[2] At the graduate level, twice as many university leaders expect to reallocate through course elimination in the next six years as used that practice in the last six years.

With the growing need for flexibility, higher education faces squarely the operating problems that reallocation generates. They are both time-consuming and difficult. It is often easiest to cut new programs and new staff, and to use the resources captured for established program and staff. To some extent, this is inevitable and probably warranted on the merits. It is also a serious hazard.

To facilitate adapting existing resources to new needs, we suggest that guidelines for reallocation be developed by boards of trustees and regents. These guidelines must be sensitive to the procedural requirements of the campus, and provide objective bases for concepts like "financial exigency" and "program need," which often become the announced standards for decisions. This type of planning is essential when growth is declining and should proceed from a basic reexamination of mission and

[2] Responses from the Berkeley Center Survey indicate that private liberal arts colleges lead all others in plans to eliminate courses. About one-fourth of their administrators reported that between 1974 and 1980 they expect to make "extensive" use of course elimination for the purpose of reallocation. Categories of institutions and the percentage of administrators who responded that they have or they plan to make "extensive" use of course elimination at the undergraduate level are as follows:

Institutional category	1968-1974	1974-1980
Universities		
Public	0	8
Private	5	11
Comprehensive colleges and universities		
Public	3	13
Private	7	18
Highly selective liberal arts colleges		
(private and public)	10	26
Less highly selective liberal arts colleges		
Public	2	11
Private	12	22
Public community colleges	3	13
Private two-year colleges	6	14

of institutional identity. A restatement of institutional goals and purposes may be helpful.

Program review should shift to departments the burden of defending the status quo.

We also suggest:

• Withdrawing funds (perhaps 1 to 3 percent annually) from existing campus programs in their entirety for a self-renewal fund to be directed to new or expanded programs.
• The provision of greater incentive for effective use of resources by altering budgetary procedures to induce cost-saving change, giving special attention to the possibilities of permitting departments and schools to carry over from year to year significant proportions of unspent balances in their budgets, and of permitting them to retain a portion of the budgetary savings resulting from innovation or investment in more efficient equipment.

We suggest joint public-private approaches to relieving the problems of dwindling growth. There are many examples of unused private capacity with nearby public institutions either turning away students for lack of capacity or planning to build. Under these circumstances, joint efforts to share capacity should be undertaken, and these are likely to be most successful if the initiative comes from the institutions themselves.

Deceleration of growth means declining demand for new faculty and rising fears about the inflexibility of existing faculty and program. The Berkeley Center Survey found that colleges and universities look to new hires as their major source of program "mobility." New hires represent an important means of gaining strength in new fields and adapting to a changing environment. Yet, except for public liberal arts colleges (a small number of institutions—about 20 in the survey) and public community colleges, a majority of institutional leaders report that they expect no change or an actual decline in the size of faculty in the next six years. The problem most often cited by administrators of all types of institutions is the consequent inability to add new programs in areas of national and student needs. As one college administrator stated: "With little faculty turnover, we are rapidly losing our major avenue to new fields and to new developments in established fields." Also, a low rate of faculty additions presents an obvious barrier to attempts to reach affirmative action goals.

We suggest careful planning in the replacement of faculty in order to avoid rigidity, and thoughtful control over recruitment and promotion. We do not suggest rigid tenure quotas. Instead, we believe that institutions can obtain needed flexibility through such procedures as the following:

• Recapturing, for central campus assignment, positions vacated through retirement, resignation or death (but not through denial of tenure status)
• Hiring temporary and part-time faculty members
• Specifying that tenure does not necessarily apply only to an original assignment of specialized field and location
• Making increased use of joint appointments between departments
• Seeking persons with subject-matter flexibility, and encouraging field shifts through retraining and through use of leaves for study
• Providing opportunities for early retirement on a full- or part-time basis

The process of reallocation and practices aimed at gaining flexibility of faculty and program require increasingly centralized administrative authority.

Both on campuses and in multicampus systems, the forces of centralization are being strengthened. Greater central power is needed to make the difficult decisions. But if that power is exercised through rigid formulas, there will be less flexibility, not more. To this complex situation must be added the fact of the growth of faculty unionism, which is likely to be accelerated by reduced enrollment growth, and whose main organizational effect will be to create still another form of centralized authority—the bargaining unit. This new, more centralized power alignment in higher education is just beginning to take

Table 16. Changes in absolute number of total instructional faculty 1968-1974 (percentage of responses)

	Universities		Comprehensive colleges and universities		Liberal arts colleges			Two-year colleges	
	Public	Private	Public	Private	Public	Private I	Private II	Public	Private
Increase over 5%	85	60	74	56	90	51	46	85	34
No change	12	19	13	13	5	34	29	12	40
Decrease over 5%	3	21	13	31	5	15	25	3	26

Source: Berkeley Center Survey

Table 17. Changes in absolute number of total instructional faculty anticipated in 1974-1980 (percentage of responses)

	Universities		Comprehensive colleges and universities		Liberal arts colleges			Two-year colleges	
	Public	Private	Public	Private	Public	Private I	Private II	Public	Private
Increase over 5%	33	11	39	11	80	7	28	54	34
No change	54	72	47	68	15	76	57	42	40
Decrease over 5%	13	17	14	21	5	17	15	4	26

Source: Berkeley Center Survey

form. It could afford administrative opportunities to bargain for productivity increases important to the future financing of higher education. It could, however, drain the vitality from higher education. As of now, neither its benefits nor its problems have become very apparent.

It is important, nevertheless, that decision-making authority remain substantially within colleges and universities, and not become so centralized and systematized that faculty and student influences, which depend on less-formal methods, are rendered ineffective in the budget allocation and reallocation process.

Recommendation 2: *Each institution, if it has not already done so, should develop an overall strategy for flexibility in the use of funds, assignment of faculty, and utilization of space, and effective processes to make the necessary decisions.*[3]

Different Institutions, Similar Responses

Earlier in this section, we made four observations from the Berkeley Center Survey which were common to many institutions:

1. They will be offering fewer new programs in the next six years than they did in the past six.
2. They will be relying much more heavily on program and course review.
3. They will, as a consequence, be making program and course changes more by substitution and less by addition.
4. They will be hiring fewer new faculty members.

[3]Readers interested in detailed recommendations should consult the Carnegie Commission report, *The More Effective Use of Resources* (1972). Several chapters of that report have particular application for higher education under conditions of slower growth: Chapter 6, "Utilization of Faculty Time"; Chapter 8, "Achieving Budgetary Flexibility"; Chapter 9, "Incentives for Constructive Change and Innovation"; Chapter 10, "Special Problems of a Period of Declining Growth"; Chapter 12, "Other Avenues to Effective Use of Resources"; and Chapter 13, "The Management of Income and Endowment."

Three further specific observations are warranted by the responses to the Berkeley Center Survey about moves being made or attempted by many institutions:

1. They intend to modify admissions standards as a method of increasing their enrollment at the undergraduate level (a practice now being monitored and reviewed by multicampus systems).
2. They intend to intensify their recruitment of "nontraditional" students.
3. They will put increased emphasis on vocational programs, like business administration.

Administrator's responses about admissions, student recruitment, and shifts in academic programs are summarized in Tables 18, 19, 20, 21 and 22. Tables 18 and 19 show that about one-third of private institutions have modified their admissions standards within the last six years. A substantial portion of private institutions intend further modification in the years ahead. Public institutions have made even more "extensive" modifications in admissions standards than have the private institutions but expect somewhat less change in the future.

Tables 20 and 21 reveal that in the past six years institutions of all types were recruiting students, with particular emphasis on traditional students and ethnic minorities. Recruitment of all types of students will become more intensified in the future. For example, 10 percent of public universities put "extensive" emphasis on active recruitment of adults over 22 between 1968 and 1974; while 55 percent of these institutions intend to do so between 1974 and 1980. Sixteen percent of the private highly selective liberal arts colleges put "extensive" emphasis on active recruitment of evening students between 1968 and 1974; and 31 percent of these institutions intend to do so between 1974 and 1980. Among public liberal arts institutions, 31 percent put "extensive" emphasis on active recruitment of adults over 22 between 1968 and 1974; and 84 percent intend to do so between 1974 and 1980. In the last six years, no private university in the Berkeley Center Survey put

Table 18. Reported modification of admissions standards to increase undergraduate enrollment, 1968-1974
(percentage of responses)

	Universities		Comprehensive colleges and universities		Liberal arts colleges			Two-year colleges	
	Public	Private	Public	Private	Public	Private I	Private II	Public	Private
Extensive	2	0	9	5	21	3	7	13	13
Some	28	33	36	32	21	28	38	31	39
Very little	70	67	55	63	58	69	55	56	48

Source: Berkeley Center Survey.

Table 19. Reported modification of admissions standards to increase undergraduate enrollment anticipated, 1974-1980
(percentage of responses)

	Universities		Comprehensive colleges and universities		Liberal arts colleges			Two-year colleges	
	Public	Private	Public	Private	Public	Private I	Private II	Public	Private
Extensive	3	3	7	5	5	3	10	12	8
Some	38	24	40	35	26	22	38	31	36
Very little	59	73	53	60	69	75	52	57	56

Source: Berkeley Center Survey

Table 20. "Extensive" emphasis on active recruitment of different student types (1968-1974) (in percentages)

| | Classification of institution | | | | | | | | |
| | Universities | | Comprehensive colleges and universities | | Liberal arts colleges | | | Two-year colleges | |
Student type	Public	Private	Public	Private	Public	Private I	Private II	Public	Private
Early admission from high school	9	19	15	15	12	9	8	19	19
Traditional	29	75	65	82	60	74	76	60	70
Transfer	24	58	51	57	40	34	50	26	16
Ethnic minority	64	67	66	55	42	56	39	53	36
Low income	35	23	49	33	40	27	28	56	37
Adult over 22	10	17	38	30	32	16	28	65	35
Off campus	18	13	38	25	16	11	27	55	33
Evening	12	22	43	31	22	17	26	67	42
Previous dropout	3	0	13	4	6	2	8	28	16

Source: Berkeley Center Survey

Table 21. "Extensive" emphasis on active recruitment of different student types (1974-1980) (in percentages)

| | Classification of institution | | | | | | | | |
| | Universities | | Comprehensive colleges and universities | | Liberal arts colleges | | | Two-year colleges | |
Student type	Public	Private	Public	Private	Public	Private I	Private II	Public	Private
Early admission from high school	19	33	40	31	44	19	33	43	36
Traditional	52	82	74	75	70	76	77	66	72
Transfer	46	82	71	74	75	61	79	36	17
Ethnic minority	66	67	67	39	47	36	43	62	37
Low income	46	21	59	25	55	18	32	68	39
Adult over 22	55	44	77	68	84	31	62	84	58
Off campus	49	35	71	44	47	9	55	76	51
Evening	43	45	77	64	61	31	59	85	65
Previous dropout	18	14	34	13	22	5	29	52	18

Source: Berkeley Center Survey

extensive emphasis on active recruitment of previous dropouts; but, in the next six years, 13 percent of these institutions intend to do so.

As measured by the relative shifts in enrollments in the humanities and in one representative professional activity (business), the undergraduate curriculum in all types of institutions will shift toward more vocational programs—but more as a result of increasing vocational programs than of decreasing the humanities. Table 22 shows that all institutions, except private two-year institutions, expect a dramatic increase in business programs and courses in the next six years.

Thus, at least seven responses are common to many institutions facing reduced growth. They reflect the desire to increase enrollments, cut costs and introduce more flexibility. As important as the seven responses are, however, they and similar short-range responses are not likely to be the major determinants of the ability of different types of institutions to come to terms with reduced growth. This ability will require longer-range planning linked directly to the situation of the individual institution, as we have suggested earlier.

One longer-range imperative is that most institutions of higher education will have to count on less in the way of increased resources per student in real terms than in the past. This is one of the hard realities. From 1930 to 1960, real institutional resources per student rose about 2.5 percent per year (O'Neill, 1971) and often even more in the 1960s. This came about as institutions paid higher salaries to faculty members and met other higher costs but did not raise their productivity. Thus the price of higher education rose more rapidly than prices generally.[4] We believe it is reasonable to expect that all such increases in costs cannot be passed through to sources of income in the future and they will need to be offset, in part, by productivity increases; that real resources are unlikely to rise by more than 1.5 percent per year, thus requiring almost a 1 percent gain in productivity per year. This will be hard to achieve over the

[4]See the discussion in "Major Themes," Carnegie Commission on Higher Education, *The More Effective Use of Resources*, 1972).

Table 22. Comparative curricular emphasis on humanities and business at the undergraduate level
(in percentage of responses)

	Universities		Comprehensive colleges and universities		Liberal arts colleges			Two-year colleges	
	Public	Private	Public	Private	Public	Private I	Private II	Public	Private
(1968-1974)									
Humanities									
Increase	36	29	38	22	44	19	24	43	16
Decrease	27	40	31	39	17	28	28	16	35
Business									
Increase	77	50	83	69	85	53	72	77	52
Decrease	3	17	2	13	8	15	5	3	19
(1974-1980)									
Humanities									
Increase	20	6	22	16	41	17	22	22	19
Decrease	20	18	15	22	12	7	12	15	11
Business									
Increase	78	71	81	68	100	59	80	69	65
Decrease	0	0	0	0	0	3	2	1	33

Source: Berkeley Center Survey

long run. One major method is to increase students-to-faculty ratios. The academic effects of this method will depend both on how far such an adjustment goes and by what means it is effectuated. Careful monitoring of impacts on quality should be undertaken. But there are many other ways of raising overall productivity. For example, year-round use of facilities might be encouraged by charging lower tuition in the summer as airlines do for travel limited to the middle of the week or off-season.

Different Institutions, Different Responses

We turn next to prospective adjustments by types of institutions.

Public community colleges. Enrollment statistics seem to indicate that public community colleges should simply do more of what they are now doing. Their growth in the last decade and a half was spectacular as they met important needs, among them needs for nontraditional educational approaches and vocational and academic programs. In most states, public community colleges are "open-access" institutions, which encourages public identification with them. Community colleges draw their strength, direction, and identity from the local communities they serve. In addition, they draw flexibility from their local form, often including local governing boards and generally smaller size. Their flexibility and nontraditional character make it possible for them to have campuses "in dispersion"—that is, to work effectively in store fronts, retirement homes, or (as is planned in "Condo-College" by Gulf Coast Community College in Florida) in beach front condominiums. In many areas, they can be the major community cultural facility. When all of these strengths are considered together, it is no surprise that public community colleges have grown so rapidly; but the growth of their numbers in the future is limited, in part, by their past expansion.

Their growth, however, has been accompanied by some problems. In some localities, the very success of community colleges in gaining financing, enrollment and support, has led them to aspire to become large, suburban campuses and to offer more traditional educational programs—to become suburban (elite) comprehensive colleges. When the public community college becomes oriented toward building "academic respectability," its concern about facilities can tend to overshadow its original mission.

Another geographic problem is occurring in certain states, such as New York, where a few community colleges were built in areas which cannot now sustain the planned enrollments. Also, comprehensive colleges and universities and even universities are beginning to compete for students more actively in the markets that once belonged more exclusively to the community colleges.

Additionally, they are faced with greater direct competition from proprietary institutions in vocational fields and from "vo-tech" programs in high schools. Both their practices, as well as their basic vocational programming, are in need of constant reassessment.

If there is a single base of strength for the community colleges, it is in their role as a community resource. Several new developments in various parts of the country suggest how this base can be enlarged. These include developing new programs to meet urgent needs, such as training programs for policemen, firemen, and small-business persons; offering programs designed to strengthen the cultural life of neighborhoods; and hiring artisans for their faculties, thus strengthening unique community resources while offering valuable learning opportunities to students. Community colleges are in a unique position to offer guidance, both occupational and personal, to large numbers of young people as well as adults, and consequently can play a special role in the structure of higher education. They can continue their vocational work, but can also develop relationships with four-year institutions through joint program efforts. Such efforts have led to five-year degree programs, which offer students a solid vocational training together with the liberal arts degree completed in the four-year institution; students can obtain two degrees and the wider opportunities that may go with them for not too much more than the cost of one.

Community colleges located within easy commuting

distance of four-year institutions are likely to lose some students from their associate in arts and associate in science programs. But the community colleges are in a unique position to combine liberal arts and career training. A group of students recently asked David Riesman what an undergraduate who wanted to major in English should do in planning his academic program. Riesman's advice was: "Go ahead and major in English, but develop a skill in welding at the same time." The student at a community college is in a unique position to carry out this advice. That, in short, is one of the greatest strengths of the community college. Community colleges are also well situated to introduce dispersed "Learning Pavilions" (Carnegie Commission on Higher Education, 1973c).

Liberal arts colleges. Until the recent boom in the building of community colleges, liberal arts colleges were the most numerous of any category of institution in the nation. But then, as now, their importance transcended their numbers. They were historically the model for all of higher education in America. Even with relatively modest endowments, they managed to hold their own during difficult times. Indeed, trends projected in Section 5 indicate that, despite the problems ahead, the highly selective liberal arts colleges should be able to keep their share of student enrollments.

The real strengths of liberal arts colleges are sometimes obscured by the romantic notion of what they once were. It is sometimes assumed that all of them were "pure" liberal arts colleges, unrelated to work or to the professions. Of course, this was completely true of only a few of them. They encompass a variety of styles. While some came close to being "pure," others were prevocational, and the great majority of them mixed liberal education with vocational or professional training. Until recently, one-third of all teachers were trained by liberal arts colleges.

The recent problems of liberal arts colleges are perhaps better known than the problems of any other category of institution. They include:

1. The value of their curricula is being called into question by the trend toward vocationalism.
2. They are more severely affected by the cost-income squeeze than are most other categories of institutions. They are generally small without any substantial economies of scale and even a slight decrease in enrollment moves them back up a steep cost curve that reflects high fixed overhead costs.
3. They are generally unitary institutions and it is hard to lop off any sizable endeavors in order to cut costs.
4. Because of their location and fierce sense of independence, movements to merge or to form consortia of these institutions have produced few major results.
5. Since they rely most heavily on tuition, they are very vulnerable to competition from public institutions.
6. Their current search for new vocational programs to supplement teacher education may attract students, but it raises fears that they may be compounding their problems by diluting their main strengths and offering vocational work which cannot compete, particularly with that offered by the comprehensive colleges.

To plan for their future, liberal arts colleges need to restate their missions, and then examine the pools of students that are likely to be attracted by each mission. Their long-run enrollment shares are likely to be greatly determined by a coherent view of their missions as they relate to student needs. Informed by a clearer sense of mission, they can more sensibly increase their students-to-faculty ratios, which now average one-quarter to one-third below those of public institutions.[5]

Although it is extraordinarily difficult, liberal arts colleges can increase their strengths and gain efficiency by sharing faculty and students, and encouraging intercampus registration and study opportunities. They can experiment with career courses by drawing on local part-time faculty, using special winter-study

[5] For a number of suggestions on "educational efficiency" see Bowen and Douglass (1971).

sessions, and developing relationships with local institutions— business, the performing arts, and the public sector. They can develop similar relationships with public institutions, but only if state authorities can ensure that such joint efforts will not result in the liberal arts colleges being absorbed by the state institutions.

Above all they need to continue their attention to the welfare of the individual student, and to maintain their separate characters and senses of identity which have been among their greatest assets. In particular, those without clearly distinctive characteristics should seek to develop some. Their futures lie more in divergence than in convergence.

Several of these comments relating to liberal arts colleges also apply to the private two-year colleges. Some of these institutions also have the possibility of becoming "middle colleges" encompassing the last two years of high school and often saving the student one year of time in doing so.

Comprehensive colleges and universities. Comprehensive colleges and universities grew rapidly in the 1960s because they filled major needs for the growth of all education—the training of teachers and skilled manpower in other areas of the economy. During their fast-growth phase, many public teachers colleges became comprehensive institutions while continuing to fulfill their original mission. Having developed good reputations in teacher training, they used that strength to move into other areas at a time when other high-skill occupations were also expanding at a fast pace. Those that moved earliest and fastest into comprehensive programs, as in California under the Master Plan, found themselves in a more advantageous position than other teacher-training institutions as the demand for teachers declined.

The declining demand for teachers and the overall decline in the job market present very serious problems for the comprehensive colleges and universities, with their heavy orientation toward skilled occupations and professions. In addition, their graduate programs appear to be having increasing difficulty competing with those of the research universities. And, because many of these institutions are parts of large state systems, they experience limited staff flexibility and campus independence. It is now imperative, therefore, for them to clarify their roles so they can gain a stronger hold on their futures. "What are we?" asks the president of an excellent but troubled public comprehensive college, "a large Oberlin or a small Michigan State?"

Administrators of most comprehensive colleges and universities believe that there is a unique role for them, but that it has not yet been well or fully defined. It is likely to be defined, in part, as a response to the rise of more and more occupations and professions, constantly more varied and complex, that mark the "postindustrial society."

The effects of deceleration on the demand for public school teachers affects these institutions in the same way as the universities are affected by decreasing demand for new Ph.D. faculty, only it happens to comprehensive colleges and universities sooner and with greater impacts. Any increase in the cohort of school-age persons, as may occur in the 1980s, will advantage them, as will any public policy actions taken to raise the demand for teachers.

The comprehensive colleges and universities also are in an especially good position to respond to the growth of new skilled occupations, and to offer their students dual majors—one academic and one occupational, or two occupational. Additionally, where they have unused physical facilities and faculty staff, as some do, and where they are located in an area without a community college within commuting distance, they may be able to introduce a community college division, as some have done already.

Universities. With the great growth of research and graduate education, particularly after World War II, the research universities prospered. They combined research capacity, the faculty for advanced study, library and related facilities, and the vigor of strong undergraduate and professional programs. Part college, part institute, they reflected the intellectual tensions and academic styles of both. They have the advantage of the flexibility of large size and the growing strength of strong professional schools.

Because much of their work is specialized, however, universities experience severe adjustment problems at a time of declining growth. Some of these problems are complicated by the requirements of state funding formulas. Others come from changes in the flow of research funds, from the effects on Ph.D. programs of a poor and changing job market, from the sharp decline in support for graduate students, and from the erosion of their research libraries. Universities may experience the most severe human problems during this period of adjustment—young scholars with long years of preparation for the Ph.D. face bleak labor market prospects, and highly specialized scholars discover that their specialized fields may no longer require their services.

Universities, nevertheless, can use their size and influence in several important ways. They can assume leadership in inter-institutional coordination and cooperation. Those in large systems can seek to develop intercampus faculty exchanges. They can bring important resources together, consolidate programs for purposes of greater efficiency, and free resources for other uses. Because of the flexibility of their size, universities are in a particularly good position to generate intellectual growth through recombinations or consolidation of units. Their strong professional schools can become resources for new directions in their undergraduate liberal arts programs. Given the still growing demand for faculty in the community colleges, universities may be able to help meet these new faculty needs through doctor of arts programs.

Their libraries can form regional ties and help point the way to new public policy approaches for better support of America's great research libraries. Their internal resources can be used to develop new management methods. They can explore areas ranging from new forms of increasing productivity to new patterns for early retirement. In short, these institutions, which were leaders during growth, can also lead in new ways required at a time of declining growth. With more diverse endeavors, they have more directions for mobility.

Capacity to Adjust

The prospects for higher education are for more than survival, but both strategic institutional planning, and supportive public policy are required to produce the desired results. In this section we have stressed the importance of the actions of institutions. Much of the historic growth in higher education has come from faith in the ability of institutions to deal with problems, known and unknown. But that faith has dwindled in recent years. Today predictions about the future behavior of higher education are more likely to underestimate the quality of its responses than to overstate it. In recent years, for example, it was widely assumed that the effect of declining demand in the market for Ph.D.'s would be that low-quality departments would thrive at the expense of high-quality departments (HEW, 1973). A careful empirical test of this hypothesis has shown it to be false (Breneman, 1975). The predicted "Gresham's Law of Ph.D. Enrollments" governed the behavior neither of students nor graduate departments. Breneman concludes from his research that an understanding of future enrollment distributions requires knowledge not only of student demand, but also of the behavior of the supply side—that is, the behavior of institutions, a field, he acknowledges, about which very little is known. We believe that observation also applies to the basic health of institutions.

The new condition in higher education is forcing institutions to seek a balance between their survival needs and their desire for excellence. In this section we have tried to identify actions that will help institutions to reexamine their commitments to their goals and their constituencies. We have introduced, not exhausted, the topic. Much more could be said, for example, about the need to adapt educational strategies to serve nontraditional populations. To increase access for these potential sources of students requires extensive reexamination of the times when courses are offered, fee structures, ancillary institutional services, child care, calendar, off-campus locations, and other factors.

We have sought here to emphasize two main points about institutional strategies. First, that they can make a difference. There is good reason to believe that the responses of institutions will do better in striking a balance between survival and excellence than recent critics of higher education are inclined to imply. It may indeed be that the challenge of decline will bring responses of leadership and imagination strong enough to inspire the larger society to seek more from higher education rather than less. Many avenues for action are open to many institutions, but there is no simple magic formula that can be applied to all.

Second, we have stressed that the possibilities for the future that lie in public policy should not lull anyone into the belief that salvation lies there alone. The survival of institutions of higher education and, beyond that, their vitality in a dynamic state depends both on public policy and on what each institution does. The institutional strategies noted in this section are not only important in their own right, but are also important complements to possible public policy. The more institutions do for themselves, the more public policy can do for them.

We next turn to a discussion of possible public policies related to the new situation for higher education. Public policy can and should take good advantage of the great resources that higher education offers to the nation.

7

What Public Policy
Can Do

There is a certain poignancy about the fact that colleges and universities, which have been glowing examples of the past glories of growth, are among the first institutions to test the Spartan virtues of little or no growth. It is not sympathy for a few institutions that, alone, evokes the public interest, however. If these were problems of only a number of individuals and institutions adjusting to new and more difficult circumstances, they would be important enough, but they would not be so much a matter of national concern. Such adjustments are common in the general labor and product markets of the nation. Many other people and many other institutions have had to make their own unwelcome adjustments, historically far greater than those required within higher education.

There is a significant public stake in the new condition of higher education, beyond the level of sympathy for a few colleges that are already hard hit, because most institutions will be affected and because the survival of some institutions is in question. And the ability of all institutions to respond to the new condition depends not only on their own initiatives, but also on public policy. The problem is national because enrollment rates, in particular, can be, to a substantial extent, influenced directly and indirectly by national public policy.

The states and the nation must consider for all of higher education questions both similar to and broader than those posed for individual institutions moving toward a planned or enforced enrollment target. Does the decline in growth reflect a compromise with the goal of universal access? Can the substantial efforts now under way to integrate more women and members of minority groups into the faculty and the student body be continued? Can higher education increase its contributions to the solution of national problems as these national problems multiply and become more complex?

National Policy-Making under Reduced Growth

Making national education policy under conditions of reduced growth is no easier for the national government than it is for the individual institutions. As we have seen, reduced growth forces choices in the decision-making process from among increasingly interrelated alternatives. Thus, in the debate preceding passage of the Higher Education Amendments of 1972, after the first financial signs appeared that higher education was no longer enjoying such rapid growth, the needs of students competed with the needs of institutions. Unlike debates during periods of growth, when these needs were seen as complementary, in 1971 and 1972 "student aid" versus "institutional aid" became the focal point of a legislative struggle that assumed high symbolic significance. That debate revealed directly how far the priorities of interested parties can diverge under financial stress and how difficult it is, with that stress, to achieve reconciliation.

In the years since that debate, the pressures and the principles which tend to accentuate differences by sorting out parties and priorities have grown. Universal access, although it is still professed to be a major policy objective, cannot be said to be at the top of the agenda for all the parties at interest. Administrators at many institutions are more likely to lay primary stress on quality, on the need for flexibility, and on institutional survival. Legislators, who are responsive to local constituencies, are likely to be more concerned about access, diversity, economy, and the ability of systems to change. Faculty members often stress the need for institutional autonomy and for faculty control within it.

Mindful of these divergences amid growing financial problems, the Congress, in the 1972 Amendments, established a National Commission on the Financing of Postsecondary Education. That commission soon determined that financial issues could be studied only against the background of a statement of public interest. The commission's statement defined eight major national objectives for education beyond high school: student access, choice, and opportunity; institutional diversity, excellence, and independence; accountability; and, finally, adequate financial support (National Commission on the Financing of Postsecondary Education, 1973, p. 63).

The National Commission's report attempted to provide a national public interest perspective on education beyond the high school. Even more importantly, the commission's analysis made clear that these national objectives were not being met. But the commission was not able to reconcile these objectives with policy actions. So strong were the divergent considerations, that, although the commissioners pointed out what needed to be done and that it was not being done, they did not issue any policy recommendations.

While the major objectives listed by the National Commission reflect real needs, they need now to be restated in terms that reflect the new context and they should include the important area of state policy as well. The complex and varied state and national policy issues can be grouped as follows: (1) providing for universal access; (2) full funding by 1980, universal access by 2000; (3) contributing to the health of the private sector; (4) supporting research capacity; (5) improving teaching in the schools; and (6) retaining conditions for self-help and local initiative. Each is discussed in this section along with our recommendations for action.

Universal Access

Although the level of enrollment is the first issue faced by an institution planning for the steady-state situation, why is planning the level of enrollment an issue also of national state policy? It is an issue because (1) the occurrence of slow growth and no growth is to a minor extent the result of public policy; but particularly because (2) there is no reason to assume that enrollment growth will end at a desirable level.

As we observed earlier, expanded access has been an important goal for higher education for more than a century. Universal access is the current form of that policy. It was the major goal recommended by the Carnegie Commission on Higher Education; it was the major policy basis for the Higher Education Amendments of 1972; and it was again endorsed as the first goal by the National Commission on the Financing of Postsecondary Education.

Although universal access is now a primary goal for higher education, it is subject to diverse definitions. One definition, often used, is a situation in which enrollment rates for the poorer half of the population are equal to the enrollment rates of the richer half. There are other definitions as well, but as long as there was movement toward the goal of universal access, no strong need for a precise definition was felt. Now that enrollment growth is slowing, how universal access is defined assumes more importance.

The extent to which enrollment rates are influenced by parental income is a serious concern. Data from the 1970 census indicate that there is not much variation for individuals 24 years and older, but for college-age groups (18-24), enrollment is heavily influenced by family income. The National Commission on the Financing of Postsecondary Education reported that although family income was not the only important variable influencing the decision to attend college, it did have a profound effect on enrollment rates. The commission reported that in 1973 the enrollment rate of 18- to 24-year-olds from families with income more than $15,000 a year was 56 percent; for 18- to 24-year-olds from families with less than $3,000 a year, the comparable figure was 15 percent.

In forming our own judgment about the likely consequences of universal access, we begin from two premises: first, given the strong influence of income on enrollment, enrollment rates of 18- to 24-year-olds from low-income families would rise substantially under a fully funded universal-access system. Secondly, in our view, the concept of universal access does not mean, however, that enrollment rates of 18- to 24-year-olds from families in the lower half of the income distribution would be the same as those in the upper half.

There are several reasons why some differences in enrollment rates across income would continue even under a fully funded universal-access program. Marriage rates by age differ across income groups as do decisions about childbearing. Persons from lower-income families tend to marry younger and have children sooner than do persons with higher incomes. These decisions contribute to differential enrollment rates. So do wage movements. As the wage rates of occupations that do not require a college degree come closer to those of college graduates, the economic incentives for lower-income young people to attend college decline. Other important factors which contribute to differential enrollment rates by income are parental education and thus the ability of parents to share experience and give educational guidance to their children; parental occupation, including inheritable ties to a craft; and measured academic ability. Among other things, students from higher-income families tend to stay longer in college.

These and other factors mean there will be enrollment-rate differences across income groups under any likely universal-access policy. The issue therefore, is, if the opportunity for access were reasonably well funded by public policy, how much would the enrollment rates of the lower-income group rise relative to the higher-income group? We estimate that they would, and we believe that they should, rise by about 50 percent. Undergraduate enrollment rates of 18- to 24-year-olds from families earning more than the median income are 2.3 times those of persons 18- to 24-years-old from families whose income was below the median.[1] The new ratio under universal

---

[1] The Council estimates that in 1974 median income was $12,900. This estimate was derived by extending to 1974 the trend in median income of the U.S. population for 1967 to 1973 (as reported by the Bureau of the Census, Series P-60). The estimate of distribution of enrollment by income is based on 1972 data from Bureau of the Census, *Current Population Reports,* Series P-20. The undergraduate enrollment rate of 18- to 24-year-

access would be more like 1.5 (2.3 to 1 becomes 2.3 to 1.5 or 1.5 to 1).

We expect enrollment rates for 18- to 24-year-olds from lower-income families to rise by about 50 percent (although not to the same level as higher-income families) for four reasons: (1) they have been rising comparatively and there is no good reason to expect their rise to cease—42 percent of all entering freshmen in 1974 came from the two lower income quartiles as against 34 percent in 1967—as lower-income family educational patterns historically follow after patterns already set by higher-income families; (2) we expect federal and state aid for support of low-income students to keep on increasing, and states to create more open-access, low-tuition student places; (3) we expect that high-ability young persons (the top one-fifth) will attend college about equally across the socioeconomic groups— the ratios are now over 90 percent for high-income and under 80 percent for low-income; and (4) states which now approximate universal access, such as Utah, California, and New York, currently have about the universal access rates we anticipate nationwide for the year 2000 for men only, but we expect the rate for women to rise toward that for men.

As the enrollment rates of 18- to 24-year-olds from lower-income families begin to rise, it seems reasonable to expect that, over time, there will be a responsive increase in the enrollment rates of young people from higher-income families. More families in the higher-income group will want their children to go on to college, if only to maintain their competitive position. We assume that such a rise will occur by 1990, and that its consequence will be an increase of 10 percent in the enrollment rates of those 18- to 24-year-olds from families above the median income. At the same time, we assume that enrollment rates of 18- to 24-year-olds from the lower half of the income distribution will keep pace. Therefore, the ratio of 1.5 to 1 would not change. The Carnegie universal access model is summarized

---

olds from families above median income was 0.35; the rate for 18- to 24-year-olds from families below the median was 0.15. The high-to-low ratio, therefore, is 2.3 to 1.

below and compared with the current situation and the earlier base-line projections.

Carnegie Universal Access Model Compared to the National Average for 1973, and to the Carnegie Base-Line Projection:

	National average 1973	*Base-line projection 2000*	*Carnegie universal access model 2000*
Ratio of undergraduate enrollment rates of 18- to 24-year-olds from families with above median income to those from families with below median income.	2.3 to 1	approximately 2.0 to 1	1.5 to 1

An increase by the year 2000 of about 50 percent in the enrollment rates for 18- to 24-year-olds from families below median income would mean, along with other anticipated developments, that the enrollment rate for the entire age group would rise from its current national average of 0.24 to 0.36 by the year 2000. Although this is a substantial increase, we believe it to be a reasonable expectation.

On the basis of our alternative projections for the year 2000, undergraduate degree-credit enrollment rates for the 18-to-21 and 18-to-24 age groups would be as follows:

	Undergraduate degree-credit enrollment rates as percentage of age group	
	18- to 21-year-olds	*18- to 24-year-olds*
1973, actual	31%	24%
2000, base-line projection	37	29
Universal access projection	42	36

In summary,

- We define universal access as a condition where (1) all college-age persons are financially able to attend college if they otherwise wish to do so and (2) there are places for them.
- We do not expect that universal access will lead to universal attendance but, rather, will result in a situation where by the year 2000 the rate of attendance of 18- to 24-year-olds will be 36 percent as against the current 24 percent (and 42 percent versus 31 percent for 18- to 21-year-olds). This would involve an initial rise by one-half in the attendance of young persons from families in the lower half of the income range.
- The actual results of such a policy are uncertain and should be kept under constant study with new projections as experience warrants them.

Recommendation 3: *Public policy should make possible universal access to higher education by the year 2000 for all those who wish to attend, beginning with full funding of existing student access programs by 1980.*

Figure 14 shows how a gradual movement toward achieving the Carnegie model of universal access by the year 2000 compares with enrollments projected by the Council in Section 4 (base-line and constant 1973 projections). By the year 2000, about 1.2 million more students would be enrolled on the basis of Series E than would be the case under the Council's base-line projection, while the increase would amount to 1.0 million students on the basis of Series F. The corresponding full-time equivalent enrollment increases would be about 910,000 on the basis of Series E and 760,000 on the basis of Series F. If the 1.2 million increase turned out to be the more reliable projection (910,000 FTE), the overall increase in total enrollment from 1980 to 2000 would be at an annual average rate of about 1 percent per year. Such a modest growth rate would ease the problems of internal adjustment we discussed in Section 6.

Figure 14. Transition to universal access by the year 2000 compared with base-line and constant 1973 projections, total and full-time equivalent enrollments

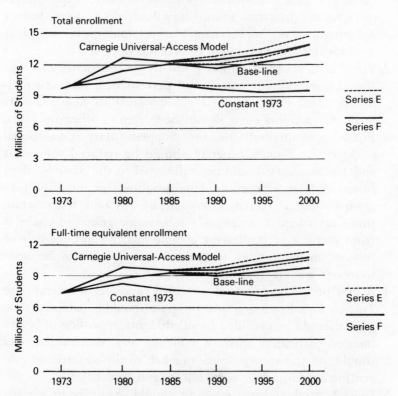

Note: Series E uses population estimates from Census Bureau Series E data, which assume a fertility rate of 2.1. Series F uses population estimates from Census Bureau Series F data, which assume a fertility rate of 1.8.

Source: Carnegie Council.

Full Funding by 1980, Universal Access by 2000

In its recent report, *The Federal Role in Postsecondary Education,* the Council made a number of recommendations we believe must be adopted if our goal of universal access is to be achieved. The most important of these recommendations are as follows:

1. Full funding of the Basic Educational Opportunity Grants program and of the Cost-of-Education Supplements program should be achieved by 1980. Funds saved from expenditures on veterans programs should be allocated to other student aid programs as the Vietnam War veterans move into older age brackets and enrollment of veterans declines.
2. The BEOG program should gradually be restructured so that the maximum grant equals 100 percent of a student's non-instructional costs. Student aid designed to help students meet instructional costs should be shifted to other programs.
3. Funds appropriated for the Supplementary Educational Opportunity Grants program should be reduced somewhat and the amounts should be reallocated to the State Student Incentive Grants program. Appropriations for the SSIG program should be increased so that, by 1979-80, federal-state funds are adequate to provide full tuition grants to students from families in the lowest income quartile and one-half of tuition, on the average, to students from families in the next-to-lowest income quartile.
4. A new program of federal matching funds for a federal-state Tuition Equalization Grants program should be adopted. The grants should be provided for all students, regardless of family income, attending private colleges and universities, and should, on the average, equal one-half of the educational subvention at public four-year colleges and universities.
5. Existing student loan programs should gradually be phased out and replaced by a National Student Loan Bank.

The estimated cost of these increased public expenditures for student aid and educational subsidies is shown in Table 23 and Figure 15. Substantial as the increases are, total public expenditures for these purposes would decline as a percentage of real gross national product. We assume that real GNP will grow at 3.5 percent per year and enrollment only 1 percent a year (with costs per student in real terms rising 1.5 percent a year). Thus the rise in the GNP will exceed the rise in student costs in higher education, and the percentage of the latter to the former will decline.

Table 23. Public expenditures for undergraduate student aid and institutional support for undergraduates, actual, fiscal year 1975, and projected, 1980 and 2000 on the basis of Carnegie Council recommendations, in millions of constant (1974) dollars

Sources of funds and types of support	1975 actual	Total			Increase over 1975 (rounded)		
		1980 Base-line projection	2000 Base-line projection	2000 Universal access projection	1980 Base-line projection	2000 Base-line projection	2000 Universal access projection
Federal government	$ 5,470	$ 6,610	$ 7,350	$ 8,850	$1,140	$ 1,880	$ 3,380
Student aid	5,470	5,840	6,490	7,650	370	1,020	2,180
Cost-of-education supplements	0	770	860	1,200	770	860	1,200
State and local governments	9,110	12,010	17,500	20,270	2,900	8,840	11,160
Student aid	440	1,260	1,400	1,610	820	960	1,170
Institutional support	8,670	10,750	16,100	18,660	2,080	7,430	9,990
Total	$14,580	$18,620	$24,850	$29,120	$4,040	$10,270	$14,540
Percent of GNP	0.97	1.04	0.70	0.82			

Note: The methods used in developing the cost estimates are as follows:

1. The increase in federal student aid from 1974-75 to 1979-80 represents Carnegie Council estimates of increased needs for full funding of existing and recommended programs, offset by an estimated decline in expenditures for veterans benefits and by the reduced costs associated with replacing existing student loan programs by a National Student Loan Bank.

(continued on next page)

Table 23 (continued)

2. Similarly, increases in state student aid represent estimated increases needed for a fully funded State Student Incentive Grant program and for our proposed Tuition Equalization Grant program.

3. In estimating increases in student aid expenditures and in the federal cost-of-education supplements program, it is assumed that the number of students aided increases with undergraduate FTE enrollment, in connection with *base-line* enrollment projections, on the basis of Census Bureau Series F data.

4. In connection with the universal-access projection for 2000, it is assumed that about 40 percent of the additional students come from families in the lowest family income quartile and receive BEOGs and full tuition grants, while another 40 percent are from families in the next-to-lowest quartile and receive grants amounting to one-half the basic BEOG and one-half of a full tuition grant. Approximately 20 percent are in the upper one-half of the family income distribution and do not receive need-based student aid. They do, however, receive tuition equalization grants if attending private institutions. These assumptions are related to our assumption that enrollment rates of young people in the lower one-half of the family income distribution will rise more rapidly than those of youth from the upper one-half until 1990, and rates of both groups will rise at an equal pace from 1990 to 2000.

5. It is assumed that, with our recommended increased student aid, including tuition equalization grants, private colleges and universities will maintain their 1974 share of undergraduate FTE enrollment.

6. Institutional support by state and local governments is attained by (a) estimating educational and general revenues of public institutions (not including research funds) in 1974-75; (b) estimating educational expenditures per FTE undergraduate by weighting postbaccalaureate students on a 2.5 to 1 basis; and (c) multiplying the resulting FTE undergraduate cost by FTE undergraduate enrollment. This average expenditure per undergraduate is then multiplied by the number of FTE undergraduates indicated by our alternative enrollment projections. It is also assumed that educational costs per FTE student will rise at an annual average rate of 1.5 percent above the rate of increase in the general price level.

7. All of the projections are on the basis of Census Bureau Series F data.

Source: Estimated by Carnegie Council. Enrollment projections are based on Census Bureau Series F population estimates.

Figure 15. Increase over fiscal year 1975 actual expenditures
of public funds required in 1980 and 2000 to
provide for additional undergraduates

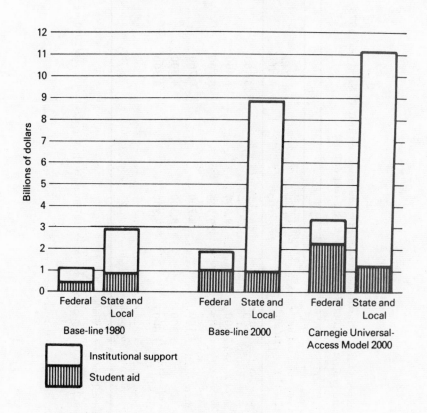

Source: Carnegie Council.

The major conclusion is that universal access can be achieved in the United States for all young persons who wish to attend college or a university at a reduced percentage of the GNP (after 1980) in terms of public funds (Table 23) and also in terms of the total expenditures of institutions of higher education from all sources of funds, both public and private (Table 24).

Table 24. Current-funds expenditures of institutions of higher education, estimated, fiscal year 1975, and projected, 2000 (in millions of constant dollars)

| | | 2000 | | |
Type of expenditure	1975	Constant enrollment rate projection	Base-line projection	Universal access projection
Total current-funds expenditures[a]	$30,100	46,400	$56,500	$60,600
Educational and general	25,200	39,300	48,400	51,900
Educational	21,100	29,700	48,700	42,200
Research and related activities	4,100	9,700	9,700	9,700
Auxiliary enterprises	3,300	3,300	4,300	4,900
Major public services	1,600	3,800	3,800	3,800
Percent of GNP	2.1	1.4	1.7	1.8

[a]Does not include expenditures for construction from current funds.

Sources: Data for 1975 are from U.S. National Center for Educational Statistics (1974b, p. 101); estimates for the year 2000 are by the Carnegie Council.

Health of Private Sector

In 1950, 66 percent of all institutions of higher education were private. By 1972, that figure had dropped to 56 percent and continues to decline. Because the absolute number of private institutions increased (from 1,212 to 1,483) during that period, the downward relative trend was not until recently a special source of concern. The same situation applies to enrollments in private institutions. In 1950, half of all students enrolled in higher education were in private institutions. By 1974, only 22 percent of all students were in private institutions; but absolute numbers rose 78,500. The private share of total enrollment will almost certainly continue to decline. The question is, how much?

In recent years, the rate of decline has been reduced by the efforts of some states to preserve their private institutions. These efforts, together with the adjustments and economies made by the institutions themselves, have kept down the number of institutional failures.

In recent months, however, for the first time since the Great Depression, the likelihood of a significant number of closures and mergers is being seriously talked about. The Regents of the State of New York estimate that by 1990 full-time undergraduate enrollment may drop by as much as 23 percent and that the "decline will jeopardize the existence of as many as 80 private colleges" (Fiske, 1974, p. 39).

A growing cost-income gap is putting serious pressure on private institutions. Because of a record level of inflation, a large tuition differential between private and public institutions, and a decrease in the level of enrollment in some institutions, many private institutions are now operating with costs increasingly out of proportion to income.

For some schools the question is one of survival, but for others it is their ability to retain the quality and programming which define their identity and which are elements of the diversity that is one of the contributions of the private sector.

The diversity of American higher education is universally regarded as one of its main sources of strength, reflecting the pluralism in the larger society. A diverse educational system affords students a wider choice, is best able to meet the highly distinct needs of a pluralistic society, and should be most adaptable as these needs change. But one main source of that diversity—private higher education—is now being threatened.

We do not recommend "bailing out" all private institutions in financial difficulty, nor do we recommend policies that will shield them from the market forces—events are well past that stage already. We believe, rather, that (1) each state should provide for the existence of an adequate number of open-access/low-tuition institutions within commuting distance of most citizens, and that (2) beyond this basic provision it should rely on competition for the survival and progress of individual institutions within reasonable financial parameters and fair rules of the game. The rules of the game are now too often too unfair to the private sector. This sector should be able to compete mainly on merit. As a corollary of this view, we oppose development of any public-private cartel-like agreements on sharing markets or on setting prices. Fair competition is a better policy than one of universal bail-outs, or one of cartelization.

If the policies for funding universal access recommended earlier in this section were adopted, the ability of the private sector to compete would be considerably strengthened. The increased funding of the State Student Incentive Grants program and the proposed program of Tuition Equalization grants would serve to aid the private institutions. We believe more than this is needed.

Recommendation 4: *Each state should develop an explicit overall policy toward its private sector under the new condition of higher education.*

During the period of rapid growth, the common practice was to plan for the public sector and, in the more recent years, to take into account the effects of public sector activities on the private sector. Now that growth is declining, it is important to develop a plan directly for the private sector, taking into account its relationship to the public sector. In states that do not now have such a policy, which is most of them, the governor may wish to appoint a special commission to recommend the key elements of such a policy as it relates to the special circumstances of each state. Such a policy might include the concept of what percentage of private enrollments are essential to retain the diversity of higher education. Is there a relative level of private enrollment below which the state should not fall? In addition, that overall policy might relate to the ability of the private sector to compete on the basis of its academic performance and not on the basis of the presence or lack of a subvention—fair play in the contest to serve and to survive; and to the cost to the state of replacement of capacity if private institutions should decline or fail.

As we observed earlier, student choice is an important principle. To avoid the danger that higher education will become parochial, we favor the practice of making student grants portable from state to state through reciprocity agreements and regional compacts. New federal support for the State Student Incentive Grant program will provide an opportunity for renewed effort to make student grants portable. Portable grants give students more choice, make possible a more cosmopolitan atmosphere within institutions, and cost the state no more money.

Leaders of the private and public sectors within each state should prepare their own suggestions for the welfare of higher education, as a whole, in their states. In this connection we call attention to "A Comprehensive Proposal for Financing Higher Education in Pennsylvania," sponsored by the Pennsylvania Association of Colleges and Universities (January 1974).

States should prepare guidelines for action relating to the growth and decline of institutions. In this connection we call attention to the work of the new Regents Advisory Commission created by the Board of Regents of the State of New York to develop guidelines for state action to adjust to changes in private and public institutions as a result of enrollment changes and fiscal pressures. Among other things, the commission will attempt to develop mechanisms to assist some institutions to close, to assist other institutions to adjust to lower levels of operations, and to provide institutions the flexibility to react to enrollment changes. This is the first effort of its kind and warrants careful attention for its instructive values elsewhere.

We also call attention to two important recommendations of the Carnegie Commission (1971a, p. 97), policies now in effect in a number of states:

> States should enter into agreements (or make grants) for the purpose of continuing or expanding certain educational programs at private institutions, such as health service schools. These should be selected after consideration of special manpower needs, evaluation of existing student places for these programs in public institutions, and the relative costs of expanding public capacity or supporting and expanding private programs.
>
> Those states that do not already have programs enabling private institutions to borrow construction funds through a state-created bond-issuing corporation should take steps to develop such agencies if the private institutions can demonstrate the educational need for them. Borrowing should not be made easy. The programs should put countervailing pressures on the natural desire of presidents to build.

Research Capacity

The broadest recommendations, affecting the largest numbers of institutions, are those already given on federal (and state) support of universal access and state (and federal) support of the private sector. Two other areas of action, less pervasive in institutional coverage but of high importance also, as public policy seeks to take advantage of the enormous capacity of higher education to advance public and private welfare, are (1) support of research and (2) improvement of teaching capacity.

The United States relies more than any other nation on its universities for its basic research, and its universities have performed at the highest level of competitive competence. The nation also depends on its universities for the advanced training of the scientists who participate in both basic and applied research, whether in higher education, or government, or industry. As problems multiply and as their interrelationships intensify, more—not less—research is required. We are particularly disturbed by the implications for the future of the drastic cutbacks in support of graduate students, from 50,000 students a decade ago to the current level of 18,500. Rapid fluctuations in support are most unwise. We are also disturbed at the decline in quality of some university research libraries across the nation. They are costly to maintain and easy to cut in a fiscal emergency. Some states have sharply reduced library support. We also believe that it is unwise for research support to rise and fall with numbers of students. States should develop policies toward research whose logic follows a course that is entirely different from the logic of enrollments. They should not be connected in the same formula. Research support should be both more steady and more certain than it has been. It should be attached over the long run to the level of the real gross national product and rise with it, or possibly even faster.

Recommendation 5: *The United States should develop a new, long-run policy toward research capacity in its universities.*

The policy developed at the end of World War II served the nation effectively. It can serve as a model for the development of a new policy for the remainder of the twentieth century.

Teaching Capacity

We have a surplus of teachers in some areas but we have a deficit of teaching in many schools, in preschool programs, for dual-language students, and for handicapped students. Many institutions are, understandably, cutting back on their teacher training activities. They may be cutting too far. We are convinced that public policies that will provide more teachers and related facilities in carefully selected areas can greatly advantage many American youths. (See Appendix E for a summary of the Radner-Miller study as it relates to utilization of additional teachers —potentially 1 million by 1987.) The states should examine the possibilities of adding teaching capacity in such areas as inner-city and rural schools, preschool programs, schools for dual-language students, and classes for handicapped students.

The central purpose of these several public policy suggestions is not to aid institutions as such but rather to employ more fully the enormous facilities of higher education, developed over more than three centuries, to achieve greater social justice, to respond to the pluralistic diversity of a nation that is a mosaic of religions and cultures, to enlarge the capability of society to solve pressing problems, and to respond to the special needs of youth so that their welfare and their subsequent contributions to society may be elevated.

The nation has never needed the contributions of higher education more than it does today; yet higher education has never faced the prospect of so much unused capacity. This is a painful paradox—useful capacity not fully used. Fortunately there are, we believe, common-sense solutions.

Self-Help and Local Initiative

Emerging steady-state pressures tend to reduce institutional autonomy and local initiative in higher education. To some extent, this reduction is both necessary and desirable as institutions and systems seek the best organizational responses to reduced growth. Yet, it could pose serious barriers to efforts of colleges and universities to help themselves and therefore the tendency should be controlled.

Steady-state pressures produce two important changes in the governance of institutions of higher learning which affect both their autonomy and the local power of initiative: (1) authority becomes increasingly centralized and (2) additional governing structures and review procedures are created.

The centralization of authority is a product of reduced circumstances. As growth slows or ceases, decisions become increasingly interdependent. In higher education, decision-making authority shifts generally from department to central campus, as we saw in Section 3, and from campuses to multicampus and to outside agencies. The new power centers in public higher education are coming to be the governors, the state legislatures, and the state agencies created to coordinate state systems and rationalize resource allocation processes. Legislative staffs constitute another increasingly important governing influence, although not so visible a one.

The main consequence of these changes is that the criteria by which education and its processes are judged are increasingly fashioned by decision-makers removed from the campus but who have the power to enforce their judgments. Ten percent of the respondents to the Berkeley Center Survey report that, from 1968 to 1974, their institutions were subject to extensive performance audits by an outside agency. Twenty percent expect to be audited by outside agencies between 1974 and 1980. Among public research universities, comprehensive universities, professional schools and doctoral-granting institutions, over 30 percent expect performance audits by 1980.

Although some outside audit and program review is a good thing, it does not follow that more and more is always better and better. An emerging problem of centralization is duplicate reviews and consequent delay. There is a tendency to require several reviews—at the campus, at the system level, and in one (or more) state agencies. Under these circumstances, even an unobjectionable program change takes a year or more for approval. New programs that challenge present methods or jurisdictions take much longer. At a time when flexibility is an overall problem, this consequence of centralization is especially burdensome.

The rise in outside influence is felt through funding practices which, in turn, also influence flexibility. The Berkeley Center Survey asked about flexibility of funds by source. The main finding is that flexibility related to funds from federal sources has diminished. Leaders from all types of institutions reported greater restrictions on the uses of federal funds from 1968 to 1974, and almost 30 percent of all institutions (and 54 percent of research universities) expect even less flexibility in federal funding in the future.

An important source of autonomy, as well as flexibility, is private philanthropy. In contrast to reports of increasing restrictions on federal funds, administrators cite increased flexibility in the use of foundation funds. As to the future, with the exception of the research universities, the expectation is for greater flexibility from foundation funds rather than for less. Private donors, past and future, are considered to be the most flexible source of funds.

Just as there are sound financial and organizational reasons for centralizing authority, both on campus and in systems, so too, there are obvious problems of centralization. The movement toward centralization, partly through the creation of new governing structures, though not yet ominous, is significant; the process, once begun, is difficult, if not impossible, to reverse.

At the state level, it is important, first, that the states exercise restraint in the application of their potentially great powers and, to this end, should be prepared to agree with higher education on the outer boundaries of state control; and second, that coordinating agencies should serve, in part, as a buffer and communicator, protecting the institutions, when necessary, from undue legislative, executive, or public interference in carrying out their educational functions.

To assist institutional coordination, states should provide a data base adequate to help institutions project their enrollments; should require that all institutions, public and private, receiving state aid, undertake to reexamine their missions and develop long-range plans, academic and fiscal; and should define the proper parameters for the state coordinative and regulatory role.

Except for a few obvious examples, it is too early to identify the categories of "bad" centralization and "good" centralization. The future of higher education depends heavily on public policy and on some centralization of decisions both on and off campus. But that future also depends, as we have seen, on what the institutions themselves can do. What they can do can generally be done better with a reasonable degree of freedom essential to institutional self-help and initiative, without which there can be little vitality in higher education.

8

The Solutions

It may not be exactly un-American for an institution in the United States not to be intent on growth, but it certainly has been uncharacteristic. It is now, however, becoming characteristic, at least for institutions of higher education. Higher education now stands, viewed very broadly, in a fifth phase of its development in relation to growth and is facing a sixth:

1636-1870—Slow growth
1870-1880—Fast acceleration of growth
1880-1960—Rapid growth
1960-1970—Fast acceleration of growth
1970-1985—Fast deceleration of growth
1985-2000—Slow growth or no growth

This is the first sustained experience with deceleration of growth, and it comes right after a period of sharp acceleration of growth. Higher education stands today at a hinge point in its history. Enrollment just got through accelerating by over 100 percent in the course of one decade and now must go through deceleration to a zero percent rate of growth in the course of a decade and a half. The hinge is set at a sharp angle. In this commentary, we have been looking at the consequences of being at such a point in history.

It is ironic that people tend to want to know the most about the future when they can know the least—and that is in a period of uncertainty. They seek for clues, as we have done, such as: the nature of the changes in the recent past, the new forces at work in the present and the near future, the private and public policy actions that might be taken. Then they try to project ahead according to what seem to be the more realistic of possible assumptions. They tend to neglect, for understandable reasons, the countervailing forces that the new forces may set in motion, like a backlash, and the unexpected, which must somehow be anticipated even though there is, by definition, no way to predict it (although one candidate might be a new wave of student unrest).

And all this tends to be done, so often, with an optimistic tinge of favorable illusions about the future that may postpone the necessary realization of hard reality and the tough adjustments based on that reality (what Veblen once called the "malady of the affections" that led to slow reactions to depression conditions that only served to prolong and worsen the depression). We note that most people in higher education today seem to like optimistic better than pessimistic predictions (Bowen is preferred over Froomkin's "Scenario 3," for example, among the prediction-makers we have listed); and that the Carnegie Commission on Higher Education has already turned out to be overly optimistic on enrollment predictions, on the rate of increase of faculty salaries, on the rate of rise in per student support, and in other ways. It may turn out that, in this commentary, we have been too optimistic also; that we are repeating the exalted expectations of the 1960s with only minimal adjustments for the new environmental conditions.

The reality we think we now see ahead, the above caveat aside, is neither the disaster that some others see nor the utopia that still others set forth; colleges and universities will go neither down to doom, as victims overwhelmed by great forces, nor up to that pie-in-the-sky, as the beneficiaries of a great new renaissance. We see, instead, a rapid slow-down of growth and then a relatively stable period, both of which phases can be generally accommodated given sensible actions on the part of all parties involved. We also see that the prospective steady state can be a high-level steady state by comparison with the lower levels of pre-World War II history in the United States and with the experience today of higher education elsewhere around most of the world—a comparatively soft landing. This soft landing is not, however, the happiest kind of place where higher education might, left to its own choices, wish to end up, and higher education certainly does not look forward to the process of getting there; but choices are by now to some extent constrained.

The new situation, however, creates opportunities:

- To provide universal access to all American youth
- To train more teachers for preschool instruction, dual-language schools, remedial classes and other neglected areas
- To greatly increase the supply of health-care personnel
- To supply the ideas and the personnel to help solve growing economic and social problems
- To open doors to adults and to part-time students of all ages, and to create new transfer routes from one institution to another
- To replace quantitative growth with qualitative improvement

But there are grave dangers:

- That quality may be lost in a more competitive scramble where the bad too often drives out the good in the "grab for bodies"; such quality distress may follow financial distress
- That control for the sake of efficiency may be overdone, as planning for the sake of growth was once carried forward on too optimistic a basis
- That diversity may be reduced as the small and the private colleges, which have lent so much variety, are lost to history
- That authority, including faculty authority, may become too protective of what exists and too cautious about what might exist; that the rewards to administrators may become too little and the skills required too brutish to attract the best talent
- That women and minorities are left knocking at the employment gates in frustration, not reconciled by the fact that no one else is getting in either

- That higher education may become too narrowly focused, too vocationally oriented and neglect its broad responsibilities for liberal education
- That humane considerations that have marked internal relations may succumb before the rougher survival instincts and so change the spirit of the enterprise

Higher education has some substantial assets in approaching these opportunities and avoiding these dangers:

- Federal support has been rising since the Higher Education Amendments of 1972.
- State support kept rising throughout the period of student disturbances and still rises, although the states are now again facing financial stringencies despite revenue-sharing.
- Many adjustments have been made, quite effectively, looking back at the period to 1930, and even before; higher education has shown a good deal of resiliency in the past, including in recent times.
- Higher education has some great purposes in American society: the education of the individual student in specific skills and general understanding; the advancement of human capability in society at large through research and service; the contribution of greater equality of opportunity in the search for social justice; the support of pure learning as civilization advances; the critical evaluation of society for the sake of its self-renewal.

But it also faces some new uncertainties, including:

- The advent of collective bargaining
- The potential rise of noncollegiate postsecondary education to a new position of competitive strength

Much depends on policies, and in particular:

- Institutional actions to assure continued dynamism
- Full federal support of universal access

- Enhanced state support for the private sector
- A new national commitment to university research capacity
- A greater application of available teaching capacity in neglected areas

The great continuing purposes of higher education and the new opportunities now lying before it have led us to call this

Figure 16. Current-funds expenditures of institutions of higher education as percentage of gross national product, actual, fiscal years 1960 and 1972, estimated, 1975, and projected, 2000

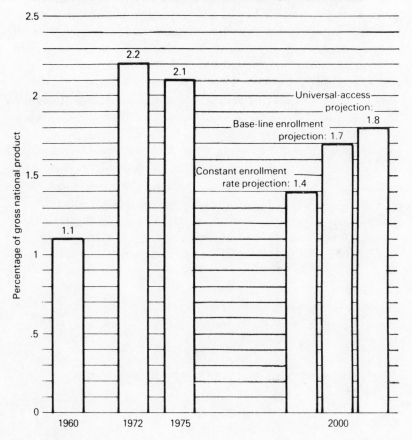

commentary "More than Survival"; and the dangers and the uncertainties and the importance of effective policies have led us
to add in the subtitle the phrase "in a Period of Uncertainty."
We conclude by noting how great a share of the future for
higher education and, through it, for society, can be written
more by the actions of man than by blind and irresistable
forces. We also note that the programs for progress we have discussed in this commentary, particularly universal access but
others as well, can be accommodated within the current percentage of the GNP spent on higher education and even within a
somewhat lower percentage (see Figure 16). More service can be
given to the nation for less of a percentage drain on the GNP.

The future holds attractive possibilities.

Appendix A

Berkeley Center
Survey

In the spring of 1974, the Center for Research and Development in Higher Education of the University of California, Berkeley, encouraged and sponsored by the Carnegie Council on Policy Studies in Higher Education, undertook a survey of higher education in the United States.[1] A questionnaire was sent to the presidents of 2,497 institutions of higher learning. Questions were directed at enrollment levels, financial support, allocation of resources among functions, personnel and management practices, and institutional projections for the next six years. Of the 2,497 sent out, 1,227 questionnaires were completed and returned—a response rate of approximately 50 percent.

The major sections of the questionnaire were: I. Basic Changes in Enrollments and Finances; II. Resource Acquisition; III. Academic Programs; IV. Faculty and Staff; V. Student Services and Admissions; VI. Management Practices; VII. Identification Questions; and VII. Discussion Questions. The returned questionnaires broken down by type of institution are:

[1] See Glenny et al. in their forthcoming *Presidents Confront Reality: From Edifice Complex to University Without Walls.*

Carnegie classification of institution	Number sent out	Number of returned question-naires	Percent returned
Research universities	85	57	67.1
Doctoral-granting institutions	81	52	64.2
Comprehensive colleges and universities	438	255	58.2
Liberal arts colleges	672	337	50.1
Two-year colleges and institutes	912	416	45.6
Professional schools and other specialized institutions	309	110	35.6
TOTAL	2,497	1,227	49.1

Although the questionnaires were sent to the presidents of the institutions, over half of them were completed by some official other than the chief executive officer. The percentage of the questionnaires completed by each kind of administrator is:

President	45.4
Vice-president	10.4
Dean	11.0
Director (usually of institutional research)	12.9
Others	14.7
Not indicated	5.6
TOTAL	100.0

Appendix B

Comparative Analysis
of Enrollment Projections

The specific projections in Figure 8 in Section 4 agree on one trend in enrollment in higher education: enrollment of traditional college students (18- to 21-year-olds) in traditional programs (full-time degree-credit) is leveling off and, at some point in the 1980s, actually declines. Except for this one area of agreement, however, all the projections vary widely in their assumptions and, accordingly, their results.

The assumption which causes the greatest variations in the projections of future enrollment concerns the role of higher education in America's future. The traditional market for higher education, as it presently exists, is declining and those who see little change in the mix of students in colleges and universities in the next 25 years project the lower enrollment levels. In contrast, those who foresee colleges and universities responding to diverse, and sometimes divergent, educational needs for all types of students, both traditional and nontraditional, project the higher levels of enrollment.

What the colleges and universities offer and how individuals (young and old) respond will determine, to a great extent, future enrollment levels. Figure 17 plots different projected levels of enrollment in 1990 against assumptions made about the nature (scope and flexibility of offerings, range of student constituencies) of U.S. higher education in the future. The first group includes the projections of Lewis Mayhew, the U.S.

Figure 17. Comparison of enrollment projections and possibilities

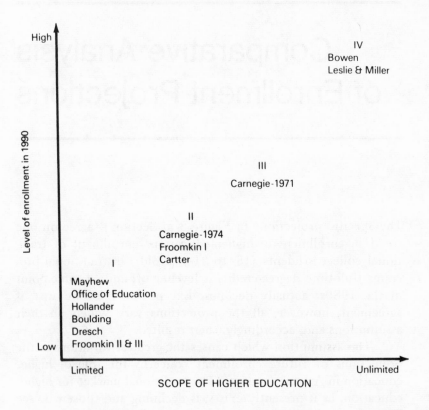

Office of Education, T. Edward Hollander, Kenneth Boulding, Stephen Dresch, and Joseph Froomkin's Scenarios 2 and 3 (discussed in Section 4).

Each of these projections is based on a traditional view of higher education, emphasizing the 18- to 21-year-old degree-credit male student, and linking the demand for education very closely to the job market and to income differentials resulting from additional education. With the birthrate declining, the draft over, and the economic value of enrollment in college decreasing, the view in these projections, as stated by *Mayhew,* is that "education, or more precisely, higher education, appears to be a static or even a declining industry." He adds that higher education "might be compared with other declining industries such as blacksmithing, passenger railroads, prostitution, or coal mining."

Mayhew offers no numerical calculations to support his predictions. Rather he cites the following factors as narrative support:

• Declining birthrate.
• End of the draft.
• Disenchantment toward college attendance on the part of potential students. This disenchantment is in part because "by the 1970s the economic value of an investment in college decreased and college graduation was no longer a sure route to any particular kind or level of vocation."
• For further growth, higher education "must attract new categories of students, many of whom suffer under handicaps of relatively low aptitude, relatively low prior achievement, and relatively low socioeconomic level. Yet colleges and universities have not been particularly innovative in meeting the needs of new students nor have such intractibilities as finance been effectively eradicated."

The Office of Education (National Center for Educational Statistics) bases its projections on the enrollment behavior of 18-year-olds, a group which is declining relative to the total population.

• For first-time degree-credit students the Office of Education assumes that 18-year-olds will enroll at their 1972 rates. Total degree-credit enrollment is then derived from the first-time degree-credit totals.
• Projections for non-degree-credit enrollments are based on the 18- to 21-year-old population. (The Carnegie Council's 1974 enrollment projections enlarge this base for projection to 18- to 34-year-olds, assuming that non-degree-credit students tend to be older students).
• To obtain estimates for older adults the relationship between total degree-credit enrollment to first-time degree-credit

enrollment from 1962 to 1972 is projected into the future. This relationship was adequate as long as the age distribution of the population remained constant. However, through the 1970s and 1980s, younger age groups will decline relative to older age groups in the population rather than increase, as was the case in the 1960s. Thus, multiplying 1960 trends by a declining 18-year-old population yields low estimates of total degree-credit enrollment.

The enrollment projections of *Hollander* are for full-time undergraduates in the state of New York. While he states that during the next six years other student constituencies (part-time, non-degree-credit, and others) could expand, Hollander does not include these groups in his projections. A major assumption for Hollander is that the percentage of high school graduates enrolling in college will remain at the 1973 level until 1990. He believes that New York State is now close to providing universal access. The present college-going rate of high school students is about 65 percent. He also assumes that there will not be significant increases in student aid expenditures.

Boulding also assumes that the enrollment rates for young adults will not increase. The poor job market and the decline in the earning power of the college degree are significant factors in reaching this ceiling on enrollment rates. In addition, for his analysis, Boulding projects only the 18- to 22-year-old population, which he calls the "age range of most college students" (actually fewer than 50 percent of those enrolled in higher education in 1973 were between 18 and 22 years old).

Dresch envisions the "atrophication" of higher education. The overexpansion of higher education in the sixties, he believes, has led to a job market in the seventies that is saturated with people holding higher degrees. Dresch notes that the expected income gain due to a college degree has diminished. He concludes that economic incentives to go to college will remain low and, thus, enrollments will decline. From a plateau between 1979 and 1983, he predicts that undergraduate enrollments will decrease by 50 percent by the year 2000—30 percent from 1974. Graduate enrollments will fall even more. Perhaps

"40 percent" of all institutions will disappear from existence as centers of higher education. In terms of enrollment, higher education would, in 2000, be back to the level of 1960. The increases of the 1960s and 1970s would be wiped out.

Recent trends suggest that higher education is already changing in ways the projections in Group I have not anticipated. The 1973 projections of the U.S. Office of Education were 3 percent below actual totals in 1973 and 7 percent below actual 1974 totals. Large increases in part-time, in older women, and in non-degree-credit students have been occurring. In addition, the headcount enrollment rates of full-time degree-credit undergraduates, both male (reversing a four-year decline) and female (reversing a two-year decline) rose in 1974.

A very major, and still open question, however, is how college attendance will respond to changes in the labor market and particularly to narrowing differentials in earned income between high school and college graduates. In a recent doctoral dissertation, *Stanley D. Nollen* develops a model of "college educated labor" to test the hypothesis that "private market benefit from college education has a positive effect on the future supply of college educated male workers, and that the private cost of college has a negative effect." He calculates this market effect by using the discounted difference in earnings of "college vs. high school educated workers over the employment lifetime." Nollen finds that "the supply of college educated white males has increased rapidly because the market benefit from college education has increased faster than cost, and because young men are responsive to the benefit and cost." His investment theory is found to be less applicable to females in the aggregate than to males. If his model proves an accurate predictor of future behavior, the narrowing earnings gap could mean further downward pressure on enrollments—"an early warning signal for higher education." From 1970 to 1972 for males aged 23 to 34, wages and salaries for high school graduates rose by 13 percent as against only 4 percent for college graduates.

In contrast, *R. B. Freeman* argues that there still exist significant incentives for higher education attendance related to the job market even with declining income differentials between college and high school graduates. With more education, college graduates will remain favored in the job market and pressures for job acquisition will increase on those with less education.

Additionally, it has not been clearly demonstrated that higher education is viewed by people solely as a means to a job with higher pay. Enrollment in higher education may increase an individual's ability to make the most of his money as a consumer, enrich his use of time, and provide other benefits which may offset any decline in the earning power realized from a college degree.

Group IV possibilities, as seen by Leslie and Miller and by Bowen, assume the greatest changes in higher education. Both view higher education very broadly and assume that many major adjustments will occur in the future. As noted in Section 4, *Bowen* relies significantly on the growth in the service sector of the economy for his view of the potential growth in higher education. Bowen emphasizes, however, that he is only suggesting possibilities for future enrollment levels in higher education.

Leslie and Miller are concerned about the "higher education function." They consider higher education to be an "essential social system" and believe that it will grow in some general relation to the GNP—"higher education grows in relation to the economy." They do not state, however, whether the relationship is a hard and fast one (percent for percent) or not, or how fast the GNP may grow. For illustrative purposes only in Figure 8 in Section 4 we have assumed a 100 percent relationship and an increase in the real GNP of 3.5 percent a year. We note, however, that expenditures by institutions of higher education rose twice as fast as the GNP in the 1960s and that this does not imply a close relationship between the two phenomena.

The *Carnegie Commission—1971* projections were based on a continuation of the rapid growth in enrollment rates during the 1960s. These projections assumed a much higher rate of participation by the traditional type of students than is proving to be the case. In addition, these projections, like the projections made in Group I, see the flow of high school seniors through the various levels of higher education as "lock-step."

The "lock-step" approach (see Appendix C) is becoming less appropriate as the participation of older and of part-time students increases.

Allan Cartter also uses essentially the "lock-step" method to project enrollment. He determines the relationship between high school graduation rates and first-time, degree-credit enrollment to project undergraduate enrollment totals. Total degree-credit enrollment is then derived.

Carnegie Council—1974 projections assume the continuance of now current trends, as does *Froomkin's Scenario* 1. Most importantly, these Carnegie projections continue, though at a modest rate, the increasing enrollment of part-time, older adult, and non-degree-credit students. In the past, colleges and universities in the U.S. have responded to the dynamics of the larger society. The *Carnegie—1974* projections, to a greater extent than those in Group I, are based on the assumption that colleges and universities will continue to adjust to the changing needs and demands of society.

However, relative to the possibilities in Group IV of Bowen and Leslie and Miller, the *Carnegie—1974* possibilities are more modest in estimating the possible impacts of future forms into which higher education may evolve.

Sources for Figure 8, Section 4 and Appendix B: (a) Mayhew (1974, pp. 163-173); (b) U.S. National Center for Educational Statistics (1974b); (c) Hollander (1974); (d) Boulding (1974); (e) Dresch (1974); (f) Froomkin (1974); (g) Nollen (1974); (h) Freeman (1974); (i) Carnegie Commission on Higher Education (1973b); (j) Radner and Miller (forthcoming publication); (k) Bowen (1974); (l) Leslie and Miller (1974); (m) Cartter (forthcoming).

Appendix C

Methods Used for Council Projections: Rejection of the "Lock-Step"Approach

For the projections presented in Figure 8, the total population was divided into smaller segments based on age and sex. Enrollment rates were determined for each specific subset of the civilian population. The proportion of each subset enrolled in college increased substantially during the 1950s and 1960s for all age and sex components. We assume that the increases in enrollment rates of older adults and of women will continue. We assume, further, that the effects on the enrollment behavior of young males of the ending of the draft have been spent. We assume that from the mid-1970s on, their enrollment rates will conform more closely to their long-range trend.

College enrollments by age and sex are calculated for each year by multiplying the appropriate enrollment rate by the projected civilian population for that year. Enrollment projections shown in Figure 8 are based on both population projection Series E and F by the U.S. Bureau of the Census. The F series assumes a fertility rate of 1.8; and the E series, 2.1, which is the current rate. The fertility rate has been declining, and thus we include projections based on Series F.

The enrollment projections presented in Figure 8 are based

on a different method of projection from other projections developed in recent years. The main difference is that other projections use a "lock-step" flow of 18-year-olds approach. The "lock-step" approach begins with a projection of the number of high school graduates and then estimates (1) the ratio of first-time degree-credit enrollment to high school graduates; (2) total degree-credit enrollment; (3) the number of bachelor's degrees; and (4) the proportion of bachelors who will enter graduate school, and so on.

Two important considerations make that traditional flow of 18-year-olds through college less and less appropriate as a model for enrollment projections. First, the 18- to 21-year-old population currently represents about 10 percent of the population over 15 years old (the population of potential college enrollees), but by 1985, 18- to 21-year-olds will represent only 8 percent, a 20 percent relative decline. The "lock-step" approach, by focusing only on the 18-year-old segment as the initial population, yields more drastic declines in enrollment than do Council estimates. Another way of putting this point is that, as the postwar babies move into older age groups, the combined effects of rising enrollment rates and increases in the size of these age groups will increase their proportion of total enrollment.

Second, with the pressure of the draft removed, young male adults currently face more options upon leaving high school. With other postsecondary educational activities becoming more socially acceptable and with spiraling costs, both young men and women more frequently choose alternatives other than immediate enrollment into college after high school graduation. The enrollment rates of young adults are declining relative to other age groups, whose enrollment rates are rising. Again, focusing on the 18-year-old age group as the initial population pool may exaggerate projected enrollment declines.

For these reasons, the Council estimates, which project rates for each age and sex group, show differences from other projections which utilize the "lock-step" approach. In their main conclusion, however, the Council projections agree with most others: at the national level the transition to slower growth has begun.

Appendix D

Funds Available
from Phaseout of
GI Bill

The amount of aid currently (1974-75) received by veterans of the Vietnam War to attend colleges and universities is approximately $2.64 billion. For two reasons this money is important for general planning in higher education:

1. It is money currently budgeted which increasingly will be available for other purposes, most importantly, the funding of universal access to higher education.

2. If the money is not used for other purposes in higher education, it is a large source of funds which will, in a relatively short period of time, no longer be available to colleges and universities.

Although it is difficult to predict precisely the future pattern of decline in the number of recipients, an estimate can be made by assuming that the decline in the number of Vietnam War veterans in higher education will be like the decline of the number of Korean War veterans in higher education in the 1950s. It appears that the number of eligible veterans will peak in 1974-75 and that the number of recipients will decline in years to follow.[1] The two time-series of veterans in higher edu-

---

[1] The U.S. Army recently announced a new educational program that will enable a recruit to complete up to two years of college credit during a

Table 25. Veterans of the Korean War and Vietnam War participating in higher education, 1956-1984

Korean War veterans		Vietnam War veterans				
Year	Recipients attending colleges and universities (thousands)	Year	Recipients attending colleges and universities (thousands)	Amount per student	Total amount (millions)	Residual amount (millions)
1956	483	1975	1,474	$1,789	$2,637	$ 0
1957	453	1976	1,382	1,861	2,572	65
1958	386	1977	1,178	1,935	2,279	358
1959	275	1978	839	2,012	1,688	949
1960	174	1979	531	2,093	1,111	1,526
1961	103	1980	314	2,177	684	1,953
1962	57	1981	174	2,263	394	2,243
1963	29	1982	89	2,354	210	2,427
1964	14	1983	43	2,448	105	2,532
1965	0	1984	0	—	0	2,637

Sources: Number of Korean War recipients are from Haggstrom (1971, Table 9, p. 44). The 1975 figure for Vietnam War veterans (1,474) was obtained from U.S. Office of Management and Budget (1975, p. 151). All other figures are Carnegie Council calculations.

cation are shown in Table 25. The same percent decline for each year following the peak of Korean War veterans in higher education is applied to the Vietnam War veteran peak of 991,000 in 1974-75.

The average amount of benefits received per recipient is estimated for 1974-75 by dividing the total number of dollars ($2.64 billion) by the number of recipients (1,474,000). This calculation yields an average benefit of $1,789. This average is inflated by 4 percent per year to yield estimates of average benefits each year into the future.

The estimated level of federal dollars needed to support the GI educational benefit program in the future is determined by multiplying the estimated number of recipients by the estimated average level of benefits. For example, the 1980 level is estimated to be $684 million (314,000 times $2,177).

The amount of the 1974-75 budget that will be available each year after 1974-75 for other purposes—the residual level of financing—is calculated by subtracting the estimate of total benefits in each future year from the 1974-75 level. For example, in 1980 approximately $1,953 million ($2,637 million minus $684 million) less federal support will be needed for the educational benefit program for Vietnam veterans. Since the number of recipients is estimated to decline to zero by 1984, the full amount of the current level of support ($2.637 billion) would be available for other programs. (All these calculations are in current dollars.)

---

three-year enlistment. Called Army Help for Education and Development (AHEAD), the program will be conducted in cooperation with more than 800 colleges and universities. After a three-year enlistment, a student-soldier will be able to take his credit to his "home" campus and complete his education under the GI Bill. As a veteran, he would be entitled to up to 45 months of GI Bill benefits, or approximately $8,000. The AHEAD program could affect both college enrollments and the amount of money we suggest might be made available from projected decline in the number of GI Bill recipients (*The New York Times*, 1975, p. 78).

Appendix E

Radner-Miller Study

In their forthcoming volume for the Carnegie Commission, *Demand and Supply in U.S. Higher Education,* Roy Radner and Leonard S. Miller contend that "further progress in increasing equality of educational opportunity at the level of higher education probably requires an increase in academic achievement at the primary and secondary levels" (Radner and Miller, 1975, p. 12). Their analysis of one method of dealing with low achievement in elementary and secondary schools—substantially increasing the faculty-to-students ratio in selected schools—produces some interesting results. They show that it is probable that an increase in the faculty-to-students ratio (for "disadvantaged" students only) from the present level of 1-to-25 to a target level of 1-to-6 would appreciably improve the academic performance of the students and that, if introduced over a 15-year period, its costs would be quite manageable. They chose this target level to illustrate the "quantitative impacts on *higher education* of a *dramatic* [their emphasis] change in the student-teacher ratio for disadvantaged students."

They advocate gradual implementation of this program, considering start-up periods of 5, 10 and 15 years. The 15-year period is shown by their analysis to involve "the least strain on the existing [educational] system and the most economical use of resources."

According to Radner and Miller: "By 1987, when all of

the plans would have reached full-scale operation, an increment of approximately 1 million primary and secondary teachers would be needed. This is equal to half of the 1969 stock of practicing elementary and secondary school teachers. Although this need not place a great strain on the system in the long run, all of the plans would appear to face bottlenecks in teacher training if all of the additional teachers were new college and university graduates."

As for the costs of their proposal, Radner and Miller state: "By 1987 the annual cost increments for all plans would be about $12 billion (1966-67 prices), not counting capital costs for primary and secondary schools. This is probably a low estimate, since we have used moderate estimates of teacher salaries, and have not accounted for any increase in costs per teacher that might be needed to tap the present reserve. Of this $12 billion, only about $1 billion represents costs induced in the higher education sector. Although the different start-up times of the plans do not affect the long-run annual costs, they do affect the initial costs. Longer start-up times result in smoother time-series of higher education faculty and student requirements, which are more efficient from the point of view of resource utilization. Thus, the initial induced higher education cost of the five-year plan is $1.6 billion, whereas the corresponding initial cost of the fifteen-year plan is only $600 million."

References

Ashby, E. *Any Person, Any Study: An Essay on American Higher Education.* New York: McGraw-Hill, 1971.

Astin, A. W. *Predicting Academic Performance in College.* New York: The Free Press, 1971.

Balderston, F. E. *Managing Today's Universities.* San Francisco: Jossey-Bass, 1974.

Bayer, A. E. *Teaching Faculty in Academe: 1972-73*, ACE Research Reports, vol. 8, no. 2. New York: American Council on Education, 1973.

Ben-David, J. *American Higher Education, Directions Old and New.* New York: McGraw-Hill, 1971.

Berkeley Center Survey. Conducted by Lyman Glenny. Berkeley, Calif.: Center for Research and Development in Higher Education, University of California, 1974.

Boulding, K. E. *The Management of Decline.* Address to the Regents Convocation of the University of the State of New York. Albany, N.Y., Sept. 20, 1974.

Bowen, H. R. "Higher Education: A Growth Industry?" *Educational Record*, 1974, *55*, (3), 147-158.

Bowen, H. R., and Douglass, G. K. *Efficiency in Liberal Education: A Study of Comparative Instructional Costs for Different Ways of Organizing Teaching-Learning in a Liberal Arts College.* New York: McGraw-Hill, 1971.

Bowen, W. *Budgeting and Resource Allocation at Princeton University.* Princeton, N.J.: Princeton University, June 1972.

Bowman, M. J. "The Land-Grant Colleges and Universities in Human Resource Development." *Journal of Economic History*, 1962, *22*, 523-526.

Breneman, D. W. *Graduate School Adjustments to the "New Depression" in Higher Education.* Washington, D.C.: National Board on Graduate Education, 1975.

Bush, V. *Science—The Endless Frontier: A Report to the President.* Washington, D.C.: U.S. Government Printing Office, July 1945.

Carnegie Commission on Higher Education. *The Capitol and the Campus: State Responsibility for Postsecondary Education.* New York: McGraw-Hill, 1971a.

Carnegie Commission on Higher Education. *New Students and New Places: Policies for the Future Growth and Development of Higher Education.* New York: McGraw-Hill, 1971b.

Carnegie Commission on Higher Education. *The More Effective Use of Resources: An Imperative for Higher Education.* New York: McGraw-Hill, 1972.

Carnegie Commission on Higher Education. *A Classification of Institutions of Higher Education.* Berkeley, Calif., 1973a.

Carnegie Commission on Higher Education. *Priorities for Action: Final Report of the Carnegie Commission on Higher Education.* New York: McGraw-Hill, 1973b.

Carnegie Commission on Higher Education. *Toward a Learning Society: Alternative Channels to Life, Work, and Service.* New York: McGraw-Hill, 1973c.

Carnegie Council on Policy Studies in Higher Education. *The Federal Role in Postsecondary Education.* San Francisco: Jossey-Bass, 1975.

Cartter, A. *The Ph.D. and Manpower Needs.* New York: McGraw-Hill, forthcoming.

Cheit, E. F. *The New Depression in Higher Education.* New York: McGraw-Hill, 1971.

Committee on Educational Benefits/Performance Measures. *Measuring the Benefits and Performance of the University of Washington.* Draft report. Revised Aug. 30, 1974.

Denison, E. F. *Accounting for United States Economic Growth, 1929-1969.* Washington, D.C.: The Brookings Institution, 1974.

Dresch, S. P. *The College, The University and the State: A Critical Examination for Institutional Support in the Context of Historical Development.* A working paper prepared for the Office of the Assistant Secretary for Education, U.S. Department of HEW. New Haven, Conn.: Institution for Social and Policy Studies, Yale University, Aug. 15, 1974.

Ferriss, A. L. *Indicators of Trends in American Education.* New York: Russell Sage Foundation, 1969.

Fiske, E. B. "End of College Boom." *The New York Times,* Nov. 11, 1974, p. 39.

Folger, J. K., Astin, H. S., and Bayer, A. E. *Human Resources and Higher Education.* Staff report of the Commission on Human Resources and Advanced Education. New York: Russell Sage Foundation, 1970.

Freeman, R. B. *Youth Employment Opportunities: Changes in the Relative Position of College and High School Graduates.* Presentation at Temple University Conference on "Improving Labor Market Information," Oct. 21, 1974. To be published in Conference proceedings.

Froomkin, J. *Changing Credential Objectives of Students in Post-Secondary Education.* Washington, D.C.: U.S. Department of Health, Education, and Welfare, Contract #0574257, 1974.

Gallant, J. A., and Prothero, J. W. "Weight Watching at the University: The Consequences of Growth." *Science,* Jan. 1972, *175,* 381-388.

Glenny, L., et al. *Presidents Confront Reality: From Edifice Complex to University Without Walls.* San Francisco: Jossey-Bass, forthcoming.

Haggstrom, G. W. *The Growth of Higher Education in the United States.* Unpublished manuscript. Berkeley, Calif., 1971.

Harris, S. E. *The Economics of Harvard.* Economics Handbook Series. New York: McGraw-Hill, 1970.

Heilbroner, R. *The Human Prospect.* New York: W. W. Norton, 1974.

Henry, D. *Then As Now.* San Francisco: Jossey-Bass, forthcoming.

Hollander, T. E. *Curiouser and Curiouser.* Statement before the Executive Committee of the Association of Colleges and Universities of New York. Rensselaerville, N.Y., June 18, 1974.

Huckfeldt, V. E. *A Forecast of Changes in Postsecondary Education.* Boulder, Colo.: National Center for Higher Education Management Systems at WICHE, 1972.

Lavin, D. E. *Open Admissions at the City University of New York: A Description of Academic Outcomes After Two Years.* New York: Office of Program and Policy Research, City University of New York, June 1974.

Lavin, D. E., and Silberstein, R. *Student Retention Under Open Admissions at the City University of New York: September 1970 Enrollees Followed Through Four Semesters.* New York: Office of Program and Policy Research, City University of New York, February 1974.

Lee, E. C., and Bowen, F. *The Unsteady State: The Multicampus University in the 1980s.* San Francisco: Jossey-Bass, forthcoming.

Leslie, L. L., and Miller, H. F., Jr. *Higher Education and the Steady State.* ERIC/Higher Education Research Report No. 4. Washington, D.C.: American Association for Higher Education, 1974.

Magarrell, J. "Enrollments: Up, Down, and Hovering." *Chronicle of Higher Education,* Oct. 15, 1974, p. 1.

Mangelson, W. L., Norris, D. M., Paulton, N. L., and Seeley, J. A. *Projecting College and University Enrollments: Analysing the Past and Focusing on the Future.* Ann Arbor, Mich.: Center for the Study of Higher Education, School of Education, University of Michigan, 1974.

Mayhew, L. B. "The Steady Seventies." *Journal of Higher Education,* March 1974, *45*, 163-173.

Mill, J. S. *Principles of Political Economy.* Vol. 2. New York: D. Appleton, 1908.

National Commission on the Financing of Postsecondary Education. *Financing Postsecondary Education in the United States.* Washington, D.C.: U.S. Government Printing Office, 1973.

The New York Times, Feb. 11, 1975, p. 78.

Nisbet, R. "The Decline of Academic Nationalism." *Change,* July/August 1974, *6*, 26-31.

Nollen, S. D. *The Supply and Demand for College Educated Labor.* Dissertation submitted to the Faculty of the Graduate School of Business. Chicago, Ill.: University of Chicago, December 1974.

O'Neill, J. *Resource Use in Higher Education: Trends in Output and Inputs 1930-1967.* Berkeley, Calif.: Carnegie Commission on Higher Education, 1971.

"Opening Fall Enrollments, 1972 and 1973." *Chronicle of Higher Education,* Jan. 14, 1974, p. 10.

"Opening Fall Enrollments, 1972, 1973, and 1974." *Chronicle of Higher Education,* Dec. 16, 1974, p. 8.

Pennsylvania Association of Colleges and Universities. *A Comprehensive*

Proposal for Financing Higher Education in Pennsylvania. Harrisburg, Pa., January 1974.

Radner, R., and Miller, L. S. *Demand and Supply in U.S. Higher Education.* New York: McGraw-Hill, in press.

Schaffter, D. *The National Science Foundation.* New York: Praeger, 1969.

Shils, E. "Universities Seduced by Flattery of Society's Expectations." *Times Higher Education Supplement* (London), Nov. 15, 1974, p. 11.

Stanford University. *Campus Report: Why Stanford Seeks Longrun Financial Equilibrium by 1979-80.* Nov. 27, 1974.

Taubman, P., and Wales, T. *Mental Ability and Higher Educational Attainment in the 20th Century.* Berkeley, Calif.: Carnegie Commission on Higher Education, 1972.

Trow, M. *Problems in the Transition from Elite to Mass Higher Education.* A paper prepared for an OECD Conference on mass higher education. Berkeley, Calif.: Graduate School of Public Policy, University of California, June 1973.

U.S. Bureau of the Census. *Historical Statistics of the United States, Colonial Times to 1957,* Washington, D.C., 1961.

U.S. Bureau of the Census. "Projections of the Population of the U.S. by Age and Sex: 1970-2020." *Current Population Reports,* Series P-25, No. 470, Washington, D.C., 1971a.

U.S. Bureau of the Census. "School Enrollment: October 1970." *Current Population Reports,* Series P-20, No. 222, Washington, D.C.: 1971b.

U.S. Bureau of the Census. *Selected Manpower Statistics.* DOD, OASD (Comptroller), Directorate for Information Operations. Washington, D.C.: 1971c.

U.S. Bureau of the Census. *Statistical Abstract of the United States, 1971,* Washington, D.C., 1971d.

U.S. Bureau of the Census. *Detailed Characteristics.* Final Report PC(1)-D1, United States Summary; and Final Report PC(1)-D2 through D52, Alabama through Wyoming. Washington, D.C., 1972a.

U.S. Bureau of the Census. *General Population Characteristics.* Final Report PC(1)-B1, United States Summary, and Final Report PC(1)-B2 through B52, Alabama through Wyoming. Washington, D.C., 1972b.

U.S. Bureau of the Census. "Projections of the U.S. by Age and Sex: 1972-2020." *Current Population Reports,* Series P-25, No. 493, Washington, D.C., 1972c.

U.S. Bureau of the Census. *Population Estimates and Projections, 1972-2020.* Washington, D.C., 1973a.

U.S. Bureau of the Census. *Statistical Abstract of the United States, 1973,* Washington, D.C., 1973b.

U.S. Bureau of the Census. "Social and Economic Characteristics of Students, 1972." *Current Population Reports,* Series P-20, No. 260, Washington, D.C., 1974a.

U.S. Bureau of the Census. *Statistical Abstract of the United States, 1974,* Washington, D.C., 1974b.

U.S. Department of Health, Education, and Welfare. *Report of Higher Education: The Federal Role—Graduate Education.* Frank Newman, Task Force Chairman. Washington, D.C., 1973.

U.S. National Center for Educational Statistics. *Fall Enrollment in Higher Education, 1970: Supplementary Information, Summary Data.* Washington, D.C., 1971.

U.S. National Center for Educational Statistics. *Financial Statistics of Institutions of Higher Education: Current Fund Revenues and Expenditures 1966-1967.* Washington, D.C., June 1969a.

U.S. National Center for Educational Statistics. *Projections of Educational Statistics to 1977-78.* Washington, D.C., 1969b.

U.S. National Center for Educational Statistics. *Financial Statistics of Institutions of Higher Education: Current Fund Revenues and Expenditures 1968-1969.* Washington, D.C., 1970.

U.S. National Center for Educational Statistics. *Projections of Educational Statistics to 1979-80.* Washington, D.C., 1971.

U.S. National Center for Educational Statistics. *Projections of Educational Statistics to 1980-81.* Washington, D.C., 1972.

U.S. National Center for Educational Statistics. *Financial Statistics of Institutions of Higher Education: Current Fund Revenues and Expenditures, 1969-1970.* Washington, D.C., 1973a.

U.S. National Center for Educational Statistics. *Projections of Educational Statistics to 1981-82.* Washington, D.C., 1973b.

U.S. National Center for Educational Statistics. *Financial Statistics of Institutions of Higher Education: Current Fund Revenues and Expenditures, 1970-1971.* Washington, D.C., 1974a.

U.S. National Center for Educational Statistics. *Projections of Educational Statistics to 1982-83.* Washington, D.C., 1974b.

U.S. Office of Management and Budget, Executive Office of the President. *Social Indicators 1973.* Washington, D.C., 1973.

U.S. Office of Management and Budget. *Special Analysis: Budget of the United States Government, Fiscal Year 1976.* Washington, D.C., 1975.

White House Conference on Youth. *Report of the White House Conference on Youth.* Washington, D.C.: U.S. Superintendent of Documents, 1971.

Winkler, K. J. "States Raise Aid to Students 25 Pct." *Chronicle of Higher Education,* Nov. 18, 1974, pp. 1, 6.

Index